African American Women:
America's Most Forgotten Asset

A'Mia P. Wright

Copyright © 2017 A'Mia P. Wright
All rights reserved.
ISBN:1973872943

TABLE OF CONTENTS

Chosen Few 7

About A'Mia Wright 9

Dedication 13

Purpose of this Book 17

CHAPTER 1: From Queens to Things 21

CHAPTER 2: Let Him Love Da Block, You Deserve Better 33

CHAPTER 3: Step towards Greatness 45

CHAPTER 4: Greatness Come Forth 65

CHAPTER 5: Know Your Worth 79

CHAPTER 6: Fairness, For Whom? 91

Bonus 115

Work Cited...148

Must Reads 149

Chosen Few

If my rhymes could manipulate the minds of many
I'd use them for plenty, not for self-gain or trickery
But to mold mankind into his image.

See the times have quickened like loans
I mean we on borrowed time.
What's more important yours or mines?
Begin to search the soul and you will find,
Not many understand your side.
As life unwind with time
You too will justify why Black Lives Matter
To those of another kind.

Black Gold is tarnished in America
They all claim they're scared of us.
But the only ones we're killing is mainly us,
Oh how hypocrisies'.

They use lies to demolish us,
Like gangs and drugs our minds so cluttered up.
Brothers and sisters it's time to rise up
The education and knowledge is within our touch.

Change was started long before us, let's keep it up,
Object to negativity that prevents the movement.
We have more resources so let's get to using them,
Evolution don't care whose choosing it!

Let's get lifted!

**Unapologetically! Who We were created to be!
Unapologetically, Me!**

About A'Mia Wright

A two-time graduate of the Grambling State University with a Bachelor of Science in Leisure Studies concentration in Therapeutic Recreation and Master of Science in Sports Administration. I am a native of a small town northeast of Monroe, Louisiana known as Tallulah, La. I am the Founder/President of a nonprofit organization that is committed to the economic, educational, and personal growth of Tallulah, Louisiana and surrounding areas. I am also the owner of a LLC that provides recreation and other activity-based interventions to address the assessed needs of individuals with mental and physical disabilities.

As a kid, I always stood out from my cousins, nothing spectacular, just different. A lot of things that children my age were interested in never appealed to me. By junior high school, I had already written my 5-year plan and goals I wanted to meet during my college years. By high school, I was star Point Guard and had set my sights on the WNBA. Thank God for realistic grandparents. They would always force me to give them at least three goals of career choices. At that time, I didn't quite understand the concept of why there had to be two additional options. A part of me thought they didn't believe in me, but my grandparents had lived a full life and knew the turns of the world.

I left for college in August of 2005, and turned down several scholarships that were offered to me due to the fear of distance from my grandparents. I arrived at Grambling State University on August 22, 2005; the feeling was of excitement and nervousness all at once. I tried out for the basketball team and was red shirted for the first semester. After many mornings of practice and then going to what was called the "Breakfast Club" (punishment for missing class or being dismissed from class due to behavior), I started losing focus on the main purpose I enrolled in school. My grades were horrible, so horrible that it was an embarrassment to show my grandparents. The next semester came around and some things had to be kicked from the bucket list. I knew what I came to Grambling for, and it was not basketball. After giving up basketball, I was depressed and stressed but it was time to make mature decisions and take responsibility as an adult. I eventually increased my grades and was accepted into the Earl Lester Cole Honors College. The President's List and Dean's List became easier to make. I soon joined an Honor's Fraternity (Phi Epsilon Kappa) and became Vice President of that non-Greek organization. I went on to receive my Bachelor of Science in Fall of 2009 and my Master of Science in Spring of 2011. After graduation, I became a teacher and assistant coach at a school in Lincoln Parish. The next year I founded a nonprofit organization, Delta Area Turn Around, Inc., in Tallulah, Louisiana to redirect the youth, encourage the young adults, and rejuvenate the geriatrics in my hometown. There is currently a struggle to find funding for a facility that is a 40,000-square foot gymnasium with multi-purpose courts and seating for 1000, a weight room, meeting rooms, indoor walking track, locker rooms with showers, a heated exercise/aerobic lap pool. An outdoors children's water playground, basketball court (covered), enclosed racquetball court, softball/baseball/tee ball field, soccer/football field, a walking track, and playground. I do understand that nothing worth having comes easy, so I "continuously strive to achieve this for our children. In 2015, I discovered that I acquired all the characteristics of an entrepreneur and decided to open my own LLC in the town where I currently reside. Phenomenal People, LLC is a small business that epitomizes in the promotion of functional improvement and self-fulfillment through professionally assisted, community based, recreational therapy. Our mission is to create an opportunity for people with disabilities to have a better quality of life socially, emotionally, physically, and cognitively. I've always had a burning desire to serve people and to inspire people. I'm happiest when I am assisting people and in that process, they feel happy and better about themselves. I have a service heart and consider myself a life coach. I am second!

Dedication

This book is dedicated to a very immaculate African American woman by the name of Almeria Wilmore Wright, my maternal grandmother. This beautiful, outgoing, successful woman of God taught me to dream, to face adversity, to rise above fear and failure, and most importantly, to throw the first punch at life because no matter how sweet life seems it's quite bitter and unfair. My grandmother was the first glimpse of God's love I experienced on this earth. She is a true go-getter. She is the epitome of a hardworking wife, mother, grandmother, sister, aunt, friend and overall individual. My Gran-Marie rocks!!!

To my maternal grandfather, Percy Wright, Jr., who taught me patience and the importance of responding instead of reacting. My grandfather taught me to control my anger and remain cool, calm, and collective in the face of adversity. If you wanted the very definition of kind hearted, you could look up his name in the dictionary. My grandfather is an example of a "Real Man", a protector, provider, loving, caring and the strength of our family.

To my mother, Tiffany Wright Hunter, for teaching me how to, despite the circumstances, be strong in and through all things. In May of 2014 my mother demonstrated her strength in the most miraculous way I have ever witnessed. Through her demonstration of strength and will power, my faith was made whole and my relationship with God intensified. My mother is an intrinsically agile woman who has conquered many trials of her life including death, and for that I admire her the most. This Black Girl Rocks!

To my father, Andre L. Wells, who refused to allow me to grow up without a father. He took on the responsibilities of being a father to a beautiful baby girl, even though those responsibilities were not his' to take. My father was there for me from as far back as I can remember until now. I commend my father for various reasons, but the greatest reason is because he didn't just take the title, but he played the role greatly. He was present just because, he was present on special days and holidays. He is still present. My father was so consistent and loving, I am ever so grateful to have him in my life. This great man is an illustration of TLC (Tender Love and Care). My Daddy is something to brag about.

To my uncle McCankius Harris, Sr., a girl's best friend. He taught me to be realistic and fearless of adventuring out to see the world and what it has to offer me. He didn't allow me to live in a fantasy world, but instead instilled in me the truth about all things. He taught me to consider the consequences of every action, but in the same instance, he taught me how to relax and not to worry with life issues. He taught me to survive, and to make zero excuses but to adjust, adapt and move on. He is a very exceptional uncle, father, husband, and brother.

Finally, I want to a very special thanks to my family and friends who continuously support me along my journey in life. I have an awesome support system, and appreciate each one of you.

Purpose of this Book

The purpose of this book is not to publicly announce our flaws or shun our community. The purpose of this book is to shine light on our constant mistakes that lead us to becoming stagnate. The things discussed in this book are problem areas for the African American culture. We must see these types of sequels as something we want to change to progress as a culture. I am certain that the situations that are being addressed in this book are not only a city or state issue, but are national issues. This book was not written to create racial controversy or finger pointing. We cannot expect another race to render us deliverance or exonerate us. It is imperative that we unite and fix our own problems. We must learn to love our own race, trust our own race, and protect our own race. We celebrate Juneteenth as if the Emancipation Proclamation freed us, but that is not true. Abraham Lincoln was a very intelligent man who loved his country. He recognized that the war would cause America to divide and fall, and issued the Emancipation Proclamation to be in effective January 1, 1863. Although, it did not become effective until June 19, 1865 in the state of Texas. His purpose was to prevent America from destroying itself. I said that, to give an example of how important it is to protect your own, and sometimes that means from ourselves. Right now, this generation of African American young adults, youth and children are at war with themselves. This generation has literally turned to slowly eradicate the road that those before us fought and died to pave for us. In this book, I am hopeful to grasp the attention of my African American brothers and sisters, and remind them of our upright positions.

I'm More Than What It Seems

Permeating like poison ivy, like poison oaks,
Once in juxtaposition with a host.
How do I get pass these judging eyes
That only see ass and thighs
Intellectual sexiness is a joke!
Who presume to quote the lines of Maya Angelou,
Phenomenal Woman in times as thus
The regularity and melody gaze pass those lies
And I choke.
Thinking of the filthiness
That my brothers wrote to describe to the world
How Queenless I could be
How Kingless I should be
If I refuse to sell sex.
Alienation, yes, isolation would consume me,
If I disinherit focus of my inner me.
My peace of mind wouldn't allow my pride
To own up to such deceit.
Queens never become things not even in your dreams
We're a plus!

CHAPTER 1
From Queens to Things

"We've all been there at some point, keep living"

African American Women have lost sight of direction in these generations. We have allowed ourselves to depreciate a great deal. The mindset that most African American Women have today effects the generations of tomorrow. They are becoming more dependent upon government assistance and handouts. As an African American Woman, today it is hard to listen to hip-hop and R&B for pure enjoyment because it literally strips women of their value. Unfortunately, we allow it and encourage it. We are more likely to buy music that is degrading to us than to boycott the industry and demand respect. Respect as a woman, and respect as a mother. We tend to cling to those things that mean us no good. Now days, we encourage negativity, then we pass it on to our children. Why are we forgotten? The first and foremost reason we are forgotten as an asset is because we have allowed ourselves to become lackadaisical. We are so content with accepting assistance from the government rather than becoming businesswomen whether it's at our own company or for someone else's company. The idea of structure and organization is far from our mind. Since the acceptance of African Americans welfare applications, black women have been stereotyped as the "Welfare Queen". It is portrayed as if black women live for and are careful not to exceed the low income to no income ratio for welfare applicants. It is also believed that black women conceive child after child to increase the amount of Supplemental Nutrition Assistance Program, she receives to sell them for expensive items. "SNAP" offers nutrition assistance to eligible low-income individuals and families. The term "Welfare Queen" was born in 1976 during Ronald Regan's term. While it is believed that Regan devised the story of a black woman from the south side of Chicago abusing the welfare system, no such woman was ever found. The mystery woman was supposedly using the tax payers' money to pay for her car and other expensive things since the 1960's, Gene Demby avowed in his article," The Truth Behind the Lies Of The Original 'Welfare Queen'." Welfare fraud is a criminal act, as it should be, but black women are not the only race that is believed to be committing this crime. But we were the only race deemed "Welfare Queens".

As a woman, particularly, an African American Woman, work ethics should be instilled in us. We should not anticipate handouts, charity, or financial assistance from the government. It is written, "laziness leads to poverty." Disastrously, many of us do not understand the formula. Many of us still have on our blindfolds, we can only see what is tangible. We become feeble-minded, and we accept what is being thrown at us with a smile. We are not grasping the supposition that by accepting assistance from the government we place limits on ourselves as to where we live, what we can drive, and now what we can eat. We must understand that by accepting government housing it positions you in an unprotected neighborhood with very little maintenance, very high risk of being victimized and leaves a lasting impression on our children. Welfare is mental enslavement, and we must see it as such. Kwame Toure said it best, "Our task is not to teach the unconscious to be conscious but to make them conscious of their unconscious behavior. Because unconsciously, instinctively, they seek freedom." Welfare assistance is an unconscious behavior that cons us into believing we are getting over with its free money, but factually we are getting further behind. This causes the middle class to work harder because of the unfairly amount of taxes they must pay, while the rich find every loophole possible to avoid paying taxes. We have swindled ourselves into thinking that someone owes us something. We are still waiting on forty acres and a mule. This is called victimization, which is something we should be obligated to break away from. Because no one owes us anything, but we owe our children a fair shot at life. We owe our children shelter, food, and all other necessities. Victimization is a disease and a stronghold that exceptionally African American women must discontinue, abdicate, and surrender. By refusing this assistance and applying ourselves to release our full potential, we encourage set examples, and inspire our children to become hardworking and accountable human beings. Not to exclude African American men who are being real men, but single households lack mostly men so the women are who the children see and imitate.

When I was growing up, my grandmother would tell me to read the chapter of the book that was assigned to the class and the one after. As a child, I thought she was punishing me for something that I forgot I did or did not do. I would get highly upset in secret because I felt as if I was doing double work. As I got older, she would tell me the same thing. By this time, I was accustomed to the extra work. So, finally I got the guts to ask her. I said, "mama, why do you make me read two chapters but my classmates only read one?" She replied, "if you only do what the teacher tells you to do, you will always be the student and she will always be the teacher." I was even more confused, so I replied, "but mama, I don't want to be a teacher, I want to play basketball". She laughed and said, "That was a parable that meant, if you don't go above and beyond for the things that are essential to you then you will become mediocre always being instructed and never will you instruct". She was teaching me independence and work ethics, because consistency is key. She knew that information changes situations, instilling a reading habit within me that sent me to college where I became a leader. I served on several boards of campus organizations, where I received many scholarships to attend and speak at conferences on the behalf of Grambling State University Leisure Studies Department. Those values lead me to become President/Founder of a profound nonprofit organization and an outstanding entrepreneur. I am very hardworking with a lot of integrity, and when I look back over the years and see how successful I have become I cannot thank myself. God placed me with the right family, in the right town, in the right state, in the right country to reach, inspire, and motivate the right people.

Secondly, we are forgotten because of depreciation. We have allowed the value of our very being to deteriorate. Majority of today's top hits identifies us as, "female dogs, sex tools, side pieces, bust it baby, and whores", placing a worthless stamp across our foreheads. Intuitively, women of low self-esteem buy into this system. They lower their standards, neglect their self-worth, and value. They look to men for validation, but the men are seeking street credit. In this instance, the guy uses the woman for sex just to proclaim his manhood to his friends and family. He even goes as far as videotaping the sex, saving her name under slanderous phrases (e.g. good knowledge, wet wet, big booty and etc). It is these kinds of turmoil that causes African American Women's values to depreciate, and increase the number of single family homes in our communities. But there is more that stems from the way we act that stimulates African American Women to depreciate. We allow these same "boys" to enter and exit our homes in the presence of our children. We persuade our children to call these "boys" daddy. We argue and fight with these type of "boys" in front of our children. As the saying goes, "consistency creates habit, rather be it good or bad." These are the very antics that the child remembers and allows to stick in their memory. So, not only are we depreciating, we are investing the same misbehavior in our children. We are the only race that is publicly degraded by our men through every mainstream media outlet there is. This motivates other races to view us as what's being portrayed on television. No, it's not just entertainment, in everything there is a purpose. There is nothing on God's green earth that is here just because, not even you. Why should any other race apprize us if our own "protectors, providers, and lovers" treat us an ASSet and not an ASSET? We boost up these rappers who speak about us in a demeaning matter. I will never forget 2015 at Grambling State University during a sold-out Kevin Gates concert, he stopped rapping to tell a girl in the crowd, "Bit**, don't you ever turn your head when I'm rapping to you." The audience went wild. Everyone fell out laughing as if it was accepted and expected. So, insentiently, that message was approved. Not only did it confirm that this generation prides themselves on foolishness, it showed as clear as day that the women of this generation lack male protection.

But just what is depreciation? Depreciation is a decrease in value due to wear and tear, decay, decline in price, etc. When I think about depreciation. I think about a car the moment it is driven off the lot. It decreases in value and if returned decreases in price. But it's the same principle we must apply to ourselves, the more people we allow to drive our car, metaphorically speaking, the more miles we accumulate and then there is a decrease in value. I once heard a co-worker say, "she cute, but she got a lot of miles on that car. A many of dudes have drove the tires off that car." At that very moment, the image I had of her shifted and the thoughts of low self-esteem, victimization, and vulnerability crossed my mind. It is the hardest thing in the world to persuade young ladies and women of today that they are much more and should have morals and standards. Doing this with African American Women of this generation is as hard as standing in the rain while it's pouring and trying not to get wet. We have swayed ourselves into believing that we are validated by following the crowd, by having sex, and by lowering our standards. But the moment you feel the need to be validated by someone or something, that is the moment you become invalid. You are somebody, and your Creator placed a purpose inside of you and stamped you approved before you were sent to earth. Whenever you seek validation look at your birth certificate and remind yourself that you are still here because earth needs you, and the fact that you are still here is validation enough.

Who They Want Me To Be

Too flashy, Too cashy

He looks pass me if my make-up not caked up

My inches not 26 and my ass not plump.

These Barbie dolls they man-made,

Wired mechanically to self-destruct.

But naturally we're drawn attractively to what they show us,

These brothers growing backwards becoming exile right before us.

Corner hanging, gun slangin, drugs, a woman with a big butt

Now he's tough and color struck by that rag Wayne flaunt.

If you ain't chewing, what you doing mentality that was forced upon us.

Girl scout cookies, purp, cush, that good good of the earth its birth,

But used against us as a tool of imprisonment.

Backs against the wall steal, sell, or scramble to eat at all,

The oppression of our men is frustrating true enough.

But why we gotta sell to our own,

Self-hatred it's penetrated our soul.

This oppression that's got the U.S. only 5% of the world,

But housing 25% of prisoners,

It's not a war that we were the inventors.

Protection and wisdom where do we get it,

If the corners are filled

And the prisons are spilling with us.

America the great

I wonder if that included US!
The hourglass has emptied,
 It's time to wise up!

CHAPTER 2
Let Him Love Da Block, You Deserve Better

"We don't have to allow the madness, be a thermostat"

Finding a help mate in life is a precious journey. To have an opportunity to share moments, share time, and share new experiences is an overall phenomenal feeling. It's a warm-hearted feeling to love someone beyond measures, but it's also a fearful one. If you've been misused and abused by someone, you've opened to believing they love you as much as you love them then you know exactly what I am talking about. It is that type of lust that leads to regret, revenge, and repercussion. It is this type of lust that leads to broken homes, baby mama and baby daddy drama. As a woman, we must know how to choose a man that is for our good and not for our sex. We must learn to use our power to correct him and protect our children. What does this mean? This means that we must stop allowing men who refuse to live like, think like, and love like real men to come into our lives. We must put a stop to raising boys because they choose to be thugs instead of men. Nowadays African American Women gravitate more towards pants "sagging", tatted, chain "swaggin", crouch "grabbing", drug "slangin", gun "havin" boys who call themselves men. We must be aware as women that men who are capable of releasing potential, ambitious driven, and purpose fulfilling do not and will not associate with these types of behaviors. Fortunately, very few of these boys are persuaded into or forced to take the role of manhood. Then, there are even fewer ones who see their faults and change on their own. Some of us even convince ourselves to look for and date men in jail, but that's not even the embarrassing point, the crazy thing is we are more loyal to these guys than our children. Loyal-faithfulness to obligation! Our children lack necessities because we'd rather put money on these men's books or get gas to go see him every visitation. We would even be blessed enough to become employed at a prison or jail, but lose our jobs because the guards are prohibited to date the inmates causing the child to lack.

Are you saying just because a man is in jail, he does not deserve to be loved?

That is as far from my point as the east is from the west. The point that is very important to life and its' challenges is: 1. A helpmate actually is sent to you by God to decrease the burdens of life and increase the joy of life. Now, these people are presented at the level of life you are on. This means that you will not find a 20 if you are a 10 and a 5 will lack what essentials you will need. God does not choose your spouse he merely presents people and it's your choice. However, when we go looking based on world views we will more than likely choose what looks good versus what is good. 2. Not too many men who pose as "thugs" are reliable enough to take care of a family, provide for a family, or guide a family. As a "thug" he cannot take care of a family because he will lose street credit if he is at home teaching his son how to color, write his name, or to have mannerism/respect. The streets will forget him if he chooses home. A "thug" cannot provide for a family because there are no thugs at school, what you going to rob, books? In America, education is key. It is very seldom that you go from grade school to rich. Again, the streets will not wait until the bell ring at 3 p.m. to start moving. Your "homies" start riding up to the school in nice vehicles they bought with cash, that will soon be confiscated and sold at the sheriff tax sale. Like any other "thug" he will take the bait and drop out of school because his so-called friend has convinced him that it's better to "get money". 3. Approximately 95% of African American Men in prison proclaim that they are innocent. This is a characteristic of lying, deceit, and manipulation. They are not man enough to own up to what they have done. By seeking a mate in prison, you are showing characteristics of vulnerability, low self-esteem, and a lack of self-worth. By having self-worth, an agile mindset, and a high sense of self does not mean that you are better than anyone, it simply means that you value yourself and you know that you deserve to be treated accordingly. By deciding to seek companionship in prison it gives you a liability. You must keep money on their books, money on the phone card, gas to go visit and purchase envelopes and stamps. Once they get out you must continue to provide and now more so because they will want the latest clothes and shoes, go out on dates, et cetera. The reason he is bold enough to ask for all these expenses with no income is because you have already revealed that you are vulnerable and have low self-esteem. Once he has an opportunity to come up and become appealing to someone else, he will leave you without thinking twice. Why, you ask? You knew from the beginning he lies, he's deceitful, and manipulative.

However, this role is slightly different for those who choose to hold the drug dealers down. These guys show love and affection to their "main chick". She gets the best gifts, and the most time. Her kids get to spend a little more time with "daddy". When the drug dealers are in jail they have hidden money in other people's bank accounts or possession, particularly a trusted individual with a job. So, most times the family regime goes uninterrupted, if he saved money well enough. If the police didn't raid your property looking for drugs or money yet, keep hoping. The choice to date a drug dealer is very dangerous. Drug dealers make enemies for territory, for materialistic items, and for product. Most drug dealers roll with a crowd for this very reason. It's not as much as a liability when your spouse is a drug dealer, its more so a risk. You are risking your life, your children's lives and your livelihood. How is it risky? You are at risk because there is a possibility that if anything is found in your house, you will be arrested as well because your name is on the lease/mortgage. If you happen to have a good job, let's hope that the boss is understanding. If someone is attempting to do a 187 on the drug dealer, it won't matter if you are in the car or house and the bullets will not miss you to hit him. You are risking the child's life by allowing him to see this happening. He too, may be influenced to sell drugs and he may not be that lucky to not get arrested in high school, or he may not be locked and loaded when the "haters" roll up. His journey may not be as well thought out as the guy you introduced him to as his new daddy. But this is the risk of raising a child in the same home with a drug dealer. Your livelihood will be at risk because you will have to constantly watch your back, constantly relocate, raise your child mostly alone and get use to him going in and out of jail.

It's not that I despise these brothers, because I have family that make these same mistakes, and I love them to life. But people we have got to be more accountable and mature about our actions, after all, people have fought and died for our freedom. Not only are they taking it for granted but these types of men cause families to fail, communities to collapse, and children to lose hope. Conformity is destroying us. We want to act like everyone else. We conform to 95% of the people who are headed in the wrong direction. We are so mummified because we want to be known as the cool one, the popular one, and the one who's loved by the block. To have that behavior is ludicrous, and I am not talking about the rapper. These men are modeling their future on a path that has yet to be conquered. Name one successful drug dealer that you know, and not from a television show. When they issued a war on drugs, who do you think they had in mind? The war is on African American youth and young adults. They pictured middle age African Americans men with guns and drugs. The fact that you target the student in high school that's struggling and allow your children to watch you "get this money" was a plus for them. For that reason, they built more prisons than school. They began to build more juvenile facilities, and the reason they allow you to sell for so long before they come after you. These men are so naïve that they think that they are invincible to being caught. But there is one question I do have after all the years there has been a war on drugs and so many African American Men have been imprisoned, how many times have you heard of the individual(s) transporting the drugs to the U.S. arrested? It's very rare for various reasons. There isn't a real war on drugs and the media does not zero in on their arrest as much as they do on African Americans. The American image of black men is that they are drug dealers, rapist, cunning, gang bangers, murders, and drug addicts. The media aim to make this country fearful of Black men, and when incidents occur that result in the death of a Black man or men the world refuses to empathize instead they mumble to each other that he deserved it. Black lives Matter protestors and are treated as illegal immigrants because America felt that it was deserving or remain silent because they feel that it does not affect them when a black person is murdered. These men must change their mentality. These men encourage our children to hate the police, but that only helps them to lack interest in becoming one. Well guess what, if you inspiring the children not to become an officer, guess who is heartening theirs to become one? Not only that, guess who will still be the target? But the drug dealing lifestyle was more important than his/her future. While watching a documentary on Black Wall Street, I heard a white man say, "in this ole Nigger town there's a lot of bad Niggers and a bad Nigger is about the lowest thing that walks on two feet. Give a bad Nigger his booze, his dope, and his gun and he thinks he can shoot up the world. And all these 4 things are to be found in Nigger town booze, dope, guns, and bad Niggers." It's no coincidence that liquor stores are on every corner of the Blacks living settlement, or that the drugs continuously remain in the hood when the dealers are arrested. It's on purpose and our men fall for the trap every time. Another thing we must be educated on is this word that causes so much chaos but, still no one can tell me what it is. Many people call it the "N" word. I've asked several people what is a Nigger, no one could tell me, not even my elders. I researched and researched, finally I ran across Acts 13:1, and within this passage it stated that Barnabas and Simeon that was called "Niger". I said to myself, Niger, man that cannot be Nigger. I downloaded the Strong's to understand the origin of the word, which was Latin and it meant Black. So, Barnabas and Simeon were called "Black". I looked up the word further and bam, the world was also pronounced in Greek as "Neeger" but the accent changed to English and it became "Nigger". We are so upset at being called Nigger and the word only means Black, which is one of the names used to refer to us. When you educate yourself with the truth, the lies you were taught become so obvious. It has been proven that children need both parents and want both parents. So, I do feel these men need love but I also feel that these men need to be held accountable. I feel that these men need a checkup from the neck up and until then they should be cut off sexually. It's factual that you cannot tell a kid to be great when you're not in their lives. African American Women need and deserve real men.

The Chosen Ones

Eyes on the prize

Full force no side excursion

We not choosing sides

Born into Melanin, it wasn't a choice!

3/5 human 2/5 unknown equals out to the Chosen 1!

Packed with power

Devouring every obstacle

Thrown at us!

Magnifying His Glory

Remember the end of our story

He stamped us VICTORIOUS!

No shade Pineapples and Lemonade

Slayed on a regular basis

Which cease to amaze me

Of the creativity instilled in this Nation.

All credit to the Creator

In Him we Trust!

No glancing back cause Black don't crack

Forever young like we got that Midas touch!

Melanin popping, curvage stopping

Traffic cause they wanna look,

Over and over again like a sweet melody

So we call it a Hook!

CHAPTER 3
Step towards Greatness

"Training up and influencing our children is not an option, it's 1st priority."

As a well-rounded individual, it's nearly impossible to look past things that you know will influence your life. It's evident we need each other as long as we are on earth, everybody needs somebody for something. Who will come to the aid of our generation? Our race is depleting itself over any and every little thing. How much longer are we going to yell R.I.P to our family or friend that we've lost to violence? How many times are we going to say, "FREE MY ROUND" or anyone else who committed a senseless crime that he or she could have avoided? Would it not have made more sense to encourage him or her to stop before going to prison, or do you really care about that friend? How long are we going to stare all the negative statistics in the face before we decide to do something about it? How much longer are we going to teach our children to be disrespectful to their elders and peers? This generation has boldly become all about me, my, and mines. Some of you may ask well what's wrong with that? Then I would in return ask you this question: What if Jesus, Martin, Malcolm, Douglas, Tubman, Dubois, and all the other African Americans who changed American History would have been all about them, their, and theirs? Even in the Kingdom of God there is a one another affair. Almost everything in the Bible tells you to pray, love, and forgive one another. This is so essential that God commands that you right the wrong with your brother before coming into His presence to pray for anything. He even asked a question, how can you love God whom you've never seen but hate your brother whom you see every day?

It is this generation who separates within its own race because of pride and ignorance. It is this generation that feel that respect is overrated and overvalued. It is this generation that has allowed stupidity to become the new cool and cute. It is this generation who embraces every trend that the media dishes out through sitcoms, reality shows, and social media. We have the tendency to say, "I'm grown, I can do what I want". This is undoubtedly, the most exploited statement I have ever heard. You being an adult is even more reason to respond and behave judiciously. You should want to show integrity because you now have the power of influence. You are some child's role model, if not your own. Now, this begins a chain reaction of nescience that makes it hard when a teacher calls you about your children's attitude and sassiness and you curse her out, as it mirrors your behavior that you have convinced yourself into believing is the right behavior, because of, "you grown and can do what you want". This is something we must revamp. Whether we know it or not, our attitude determines our altitude. You can be the "grownest" person on the face of the earth, but at some point, in your life, and in some cases at several points, you will need someone that is not a family or friend. A lot of times you end up needing that very person you called every defiling word in your vocabulary the most. In life, if you want to evolve at anything, your attitude will determine your elaboration. We've been "poppin off", "cutting up", "piping it up" and "going hard" on people for as long as I can remember, and all it has gotten us is another label "mad black woman", a charge of assault, and a broken family by losing someone to death or murder case. So how long are we going to continue to do the same thing that produces zero progress? I once heard a man say, "a fool is someone who is consistent in doing the same exact thing, but hoping for different results."

What we must understand as a young generation is that racism still exist, in America. Discrimination is still a key component in this country. We still start off with strike one because of the color of our skin. Many people want this to be overlooked but we cannot forget the founding 246 years of which our ancestors fought and died. Those 246 years is evidence of our strength, our courage, and our ability to overcome. Unfortunately, those 246 years took a lot of lives through hatred, but nonetheless, we have evolved into a phenomenal people. Because of this it is hard for us to advance above what is expected of us in this country. There are very slim chances that we become more than athletes, artist, entertainers, or drug dealers. This is the norm that was created for us. So, teaching our children to be disrespectful, grown, and to have negative attitudes only sets them up for failure. You are lethargically digging a hole for them to fall into. We are a great asset to our children. It is our job to prepare them and equip them with the necessary tools to succeed in life. It is the mother's responsibility to disciple and to teach integrity, morals and values to our children. If our children are disruptive at home, why would you fault the teacher for contacting you concerning your child boldly talking back or having problems following directives. Your child is only at school eight hours a day; it is impossible to teach a curriculum and mannerism and it's simply not their jobs. The parent and the teacher should be on one accord. Yes, there are some teachers with hidden motives and childish ways that pick with the child because of who the child's parents are or because of the child's attitude. No, this is not right, but a way to fix this is to create a healthy relationship with your child, and every day ask about what happened at school in general to be aware. As a mother, you should know what bad habits your child has, if there is something that a teacher says he or she has done that is out of the norm just begin to visit the class, schedule meetings, and make it clear that you are actively involved in your child's life. The one thing you should never do is express your thoughts about the teacher in front of your child, because that alerts the child that you dislike the teacher and is indirectly a pass for them to disrespect her. We have become customary to celebrating when our children graduate high school and college as if accomplishing these things are rare for our culture. We should celebrate because that child has done his or her due diligence. This is another negative spotlight that the media heightens. This is common to our ancestors, in fact, they opened many institutions for blacks. It is rare now, because intuitively we've accepted what the media showed us, that blacks are uneducated. In Tulsa, Oklahoma there was many blacks rising and operated within their own small region called Greenwood. In Black Wall Street as it was called by blacks and little Africa as it was called by Whites there were over 150 black owned businesses, hospitals, schools, and churches. In 1921, the growing and throbbing town was destroyed by a race riot. 300 blacks were killed. They looted and burned 40 square blocks of 1,265 African American homes, businesses, hospitals, and all the churches except one, uncommonly it was on the White side of town. The whites were looting the black's homes and wearing the clothes that they had taken. One interviewee stated that a white woman told her that these "Niggers have better things than we have." 6,000 blacks were arrested and detained by the National Guard although they were the ones being attacked. There were 1,400 claims made, but not one black person was paid, however, one claim was paid to a white store owner who stated that his guns and ammo was stolen by Whites. The blacks returned only to find that all that they worked so hard for was burned completely down, and many of the bricks were stolen. In December of 1921 the citizens of Greenwood placed a large tree in the center of town and over 2,200 gathered on Christmas day and began to sing carols and Negro spirituals that attracted much attention, said Maurice Willis, Director of the Red

Cross, 1921. I guess the movie "How the Grinch Stole Christmas" stole more than Christmas, they stole that scene from Black Wall Street. They deemed us lazy, yet we built the country. A slaves' work day was from sunrise to sunset everyday but Sunday, if the slave owner was religious. They told us that we were illiterate, but so was the first person that learned to read. Governor George Wallace once stated that, "whites did not care if they lacked homes, land, or hospitals they just wanted to know that they were better than blacks." None of it was true or could be proven. But we slowly bought into that foolishness and began to drop out of school at the slightest face of difficulty. We are becoming lazy and dependent upon the government. We now destroy each other, and some of us just simply hate his/her own skin. It is all a result of being broken into a million pieces and put back together with bandages that were tainted with hate, lies and deceit. It is a result of being stripped naked mentally and physically as a nation. My grandmother always told me to find some good in everything you go through, seek God's face in everything. After research, after reading books upon books, watching documentaries and listening to my elders one word dinged "volatile". As a race, we are strong. We are effervescent, and we are buoyant. We have no reason to hang our heads, and the good thing about it is that the best is still yet to come.

What does justice look like for blacks? How much of a threat is our skin? The cognitive dissonance associated with them killing us is that we are not human but merely wild animals, beast of the fields. Killing us is called gaming. They are emotionally, socially, and cognitively detached from viewing us as people too. That is the reason we are being slaughtered, and they are awarded. In the hood, there is a G-code that everybody involuntarily abides by. One of the procedures within the G-code is that you are forbidden to snitch. This is the dumbest rule I've ever heard of to be exact. Our neighborhoods are viewed as the lowest point of humane society. The government use our neighborhoods as traps, and we are lab rats. People can come to our communities and buy drugs, abuse drugs, kill, fight and whatever else all while our children watching. We refuse to put a stop to incidents like this or find a well-respected cop to patrol our community to put a halt to the nonsense. We think we are fitting in by turning our heads or refusing to speak out on one of our own being murdered. Frankly, it's ignorant and declares a war against our own. It's no better than those who remain silent to police brutality. White people will come to our neighborhood for drugs, but you will serve 25 to life, figuratively speaking, if you went into a white neighborhood trying to sell drugs. Because it is important, they are going to protect their children and their family. Although, there are way more White drug dealers and users than black, the only time their children see someone selling drugs or abusing them is when they turn on the television and quite naturally it's us that's selling them according to the mainstream media. We sell drugs and abuse drugs in front of our children, then some of us go as far as sharing it with them. We convince ourselves that being high helps us cope with life, when truly it prevents us from getting a job, prevents us from maximizing our potential, and it causes us to lose brain cells. Being a mother is the most important job on earth, yet the most rewarding. Nikita Venzant, described it as the best feeling in the world, "it's amazing to have a person that will love you forever regardless it's an indescribable feeling," she said. Women are so important to God that He chose us to be His very own agents here on earth. He trusts us to populate the earth and deliver greatness. A child can be born without the presence of a father but a child cannot be born without a mother. If we are that valuable to God, why are we nothing to men? Why do we allow ourselves to be misused and abused? We must remind ourselves that the most valuable gifts have the hardest task, and what is more painful than child birth. No, we are not greater, but we are not less either. We are God's agents on earth, we are more influential and powerful than we are accredited for. When we realize how important we are we will begin to pour that energy into our youth. We will begin to make better decisions when choosing a spouse, and we will make better decisions for our future. This is not impossible, altering our intellectual being, it's a matter of wanting to be the change our culture needs. The media makes it plain to see that our people need a change. Tupac said it 20 years ago, "let's change the way we eat, let's change the way we live, and let's change the way we treat each other." It's 20 years later and it has gotten worse, we are being led by the biggest liar ever, the media.

We are screaming "Black Lives Matter" well let's focus on exhausting all opportunities to keep our children out of the streets which gives the authorities less occurrences to approach us. If black lives matter, why do we promote these artists that influence black on black crime, drugs, and banging? It is our youth who are listening to this madness they now call music with the intentions to live the life these artists rap about. It is our youth who fail to realize that the music is for entertainment, and not to be mimicked. We must teach our children the different stereotypes to help them shy away from labels and statistics that leave a negative stamp. We are raising our boys as our "lil shooters", the only thing we are helping them be are targets. "The Savage" stereotype was established in 1915. Racial violence picked up heavily and it was justified and encouraged through the emphasis on this stereotype of "the savage". The urgent messages to whites were, we must put blacks in their place or else (Boskin, 1986). The animal-like savage stereotype was used to rationalize the harsh treatment of our ancestors in slavery times, also murder, torture, and oppression stated by Laura Green in her article, Stereotypes: Negative Racial Stereotypes and Their Effect on Attitudes Toward African-Americans. We should inform our children of "The Causal Killing Act", this law protected Whites who were beating blacks to correct them, the assurance that if perhaps we died during that beating, then they would be acquitted and they will not be charged. What's ironic is it was the White women who were beating black children to death. We should teach our children that slavery was not that long ago, and lynching occurred after slavery. Ida Wells was a well-known journalist who reported that there were 1,217 African Americans who had been lynched between the years of 1890 and 1900. I must remind you that "slavery" supposedly ended in 1863 with the signing of the Emancipation Proclamation. Because of the constantly wrongful killings of African Americans in 1909, the NAACP (National Association for the Advancement of Colored People) was formed, but the significance of the organization is that it was started by Whites whom genuinely cared and had empathy for African Americans. The NAACP was founded by Mary White Ovington, Oswald Garrison Villard, William English Walling and Dr. Henry Moscowitz who were all white. Ida Wells-Barnett and W.E.B DuBois who were black. There was not a black president of the

NAACP until 1975, which was W.E.B DuBois whom was the only non-white national officer. This is important because the media has lead the people to believe that the NAACP is an anti-white organization that focus on destroying whites and building up blacks, completely miseducation of what the NAACP stands for. The NAACP has a rule that shuts down that lie altogether, you cannot even form a chapter unless you have the equal amount of whites and blacks. For instance, ten black people could not start a local chapter unless there were ten white people interested in starting a local chapter with them and vice versa. But unless you are interested and research the truth, the lie you were told will keep you in a box. We should never be afraid to learn about African American History; our history speaks volumes to our action and responses today. When we begin to understand that applied knowledge is power we will begin to grow enormously. We are so lost as a race that we voluntarily break each other down because of the shades of our skin. We are so wrapped up and consumed by what appears to the naked eye that we miss out on the greatest gift of all. The world feeds us that our history begins in 1619, we never stopped to question who we really are, or who we were before we were kidnapped and dropped off in a place they called "New World". We never took the time to research why our ancestors used the word "Massa" instead of "Master". We didn't have time to find out that "Massa" in Hebrew means oppressor. We only mocked what the media showed us. As a mother/guardian these are crucial to know so that we can pass down for future generations. We should teach our children about the stereotype "Sambo" and "Jim Crow". If we know where we come from, then we will know how to plan to successfully get where we are going. It is puzzling to me how all the potent information about African Americans somehow vanished into thin air. Geographically, there is no such thing as the Middle East, if so, where is the Middle West or Middle North? However, Israel which is geographically located in northeast Africa is middle east to Europe, but admitting this will raise questions about the Bible. If we are blind to from whence we came, then we will continue to make a circle, falling for the same trickery, landing in the same hole, and playing the same puppet on a string. My 12th grade English teacher, Mrs. Nancy Johnson, use to always tell us, "when you know better, you do better". She would come back to say, "Ray Charles can't lead Stevie Wonder." As long as we continue to remain ignorant to who we are, what we are here for, where we come from, why us, and when we will change it, everything will continue to be null and void to us. Just ask yourself these same questions, and use the answers American History gave us then analyze to see what sense it makes to you.

> ***Who?*** *They say we are Africans from Africa. Well, Africa is the second largest continent in the world with fifty-four (54) individual countries. Which one? You mean to tell me you boldly entered the second largest continent in the world and just started kidnapping people? So, you captured approximately fifteen million Africans and no one tried stopping you in their own homeland? You mean to tell me that Africans were selling Africans? Well, why aren't we accepted as Africans by Africans?* ***What are we here for?*** *Slavery? Deuteronomy 28 says differently. The chapter is rather lengthy but I challenge you to read it, not in a religious viewpoint but in a historical viewpoint and I guarantee you discover the slave trade just as I did.* ***Where did we come from?*** *West Africa they say. Research shows that the people sold in West Africa (Benin) at La Porte Du Non-Retour-Door of No Return were not Africans, and were said to be outsiders by the West Africans and Grecians. Those individuals were said to be the real Israelites/Hebrews. So, we may want to research to see which of 10 Lost Tribes of Israel we belong to.* ***Why us?*** *Have you ever thought what is so special about us that it was imperative that we forget our history so much so that even our name was stripped from us? Now, ask yourself if you were nothing or nobody, swinging in trees and scratching your behind, what would it matter if you knew who you were? But, if you were everything I longed to be, who you are, would be the first thing I'd destroy to restore a mindset of inferiority. It's*

like a controlling relationship the dominate individual when incompetent of having a free and healthy relationship, does things to tear down their lover's self-esteem, character, and the overall individual to gain and keep control. To destroy the mind is to gain the individual. **When will we change?** *When we build a foundation of who we are, love ourselves enough to change, and create unity progress will become automatic. Confusion caused nations to divide, you have to know who you are to know where you are going. True love conquers all, love bore stripes, healed the land and conquered the grave and in three (3) days love rose and told Mary (a woman) to tell the others that "I AM" has arisen just as he said. We cannot overcome this without love for each other and for our purpose. We will need unity as it creates strengths, bonds, opportunities, and threats.*

We struggle mentally because we do not know who we are, so we act out. If you have ever gone to counseling or so much of seen someone being counseled on television, the first statement the Counselor utters is, "Well, let's get to the root of the problem." We cannot dig that deep without the information being tainted, destroyed, or beguiled. Pinckney Benton Stewart Pinchback, once spoke with great authority, he reminded African Americans of the power they could wield as a coalition: "With this force as a political element, as laborers, producers, and consumers, we are an element of strength and wealth too powerful to be ignored" written in "100 African Americans who changed History" book. African American Women I speak to you with that same authority today, we are too powerful to be ignored, used, abused and done away with! Let's be who we were created to be, let's get back to raising our children to fear God, let's get back to the days of respect and mannerism, WOMEN LET'S GET BACK TO OUR UPRIGHT POSITIONS AS CHILDREN OF THE MOST HIGH!

Power Creates Fear

Female Revolutionaries you should know
Kathleen Cleaver, Angela Davis and Assata Shakur
to name a few of the flaming stars.
Elaine Brown, Barbara Easley, and Charlotte Hill O'Neal
just to spill the knowledge that they want concealed.
Tarika Matilaba, Judy Hart, and Chaka Khan
possessed many talents but the media only revealed one!
Many of these women had to flee the country
and are said to be notorious
Never once convicted but acquitted of all the charges!
Evolution of the movement
That they were choosing
Black Panther Party it took a Bruisin'!
They were falsely accusing
And placing people under the elusion
That these people were starting confusion
But actually they were loosening the mental chains
And strains of a bias constitution
By refusing to remain helpless and lame.
It's a shame how the Government and media play petty games,
Hot mess so we just stress
Cause we just guess
If we sit idle and say we bless
It'll all change.

But they power trip so don't ever slip,
Thinking they'll loosen the reigns.

CHAPTER 4
Greatness Come Forth

"Go down and tell Pharaoh, let my people go!"

Today, much of our great works are burned and buried. We feel inferior to other races. We doubt ourselves based on what we see. We forget that God told us faith comes by hearing and receiving the Word. Faith is expressed by works and without work faith is dead. So, Faith is manifested by heart's conviction plus mouth confession. We forget that the Bible tells us that we can do all things through Christ who strengthens us. We quickly forget that the Bible tells us that we are a skillful people, a Royal Priesthood, a peculiar people and a child of the most-high

God. We forget these things because most of our day is devoted to social media, television, and becoming a statistic. We forget these things because we only hear the Word being told by someone else once a week for an hour or two. We forget these things because sometimes that one who is giving the Word found church to be a business and his focus is to get paid. We have gone through generations of trauma and so much so that the training our ancestors received on how to address Whites, how to dress properly for Whites, or even how to be respectful even when you are being treated as an adolescent(disrespected). Still to this very day, we react in a certain matter when we are interacting with Whites. We are yearning for attention when we are to them invisible. We were considered incapable of thinking for ourselves, so we only do what we are told to do. We were considered incapable of being responsible adults so we were placed in ghettos, on food stamps, restricted to become independent adults or risk losing all government assistance. The men were placed in jail for being an illegitimate father (child support), drugs, loitering and even old or no charge at all. Simply because they deemed us incapable, inhumane, and too illiterate to understand the laws that were to be governing by. But it is evident that we can overcome the stereotypes, labels, and negative perception that has branded us. We have evolved from being called Sapphires, Jezebel's, Mammy, Aunt Jemima, and Welfare Queens to a platform of authors, scholars, actresses, athletes, businesswomen, lawyers, and the list ceases to expire. Just when we thought we had reached the top of the totem pole, one of us reached the White House as the First Lady and not a maid. Our First Lady has influenced many and proved her doubters to be miscalculated. She became the face of health and wellness. She even reconstructed the meals that affect our children. This became a door that the media tried to use as a weapon. To many parents unbeknownst, the U.S. is the unhealthiest country in the world, obesity is ruining our children(s) childhood. African Americans rank the highest in diabetes, high cholesterol, high blood pressure, and obesity. This was needed to give our youth and children an opportunity to experience longevity. There is greatness in each one of us. Some people have a harder time tapping into theirs than others but it's there. I truly believe that African American people are very resilient people, to be more precise I believe that we were strategically designed to be overcomers, victorious, conquers, powerful, and every other word that reflects our strength. But we had to go through the journey to write the story and proclaim it. There is not one race that has gone through or is still enduring the things that people of African descent has and is bearing. Yes, racism has always been around but not at the level that America enslaved African Americans. No one else! God is so good! Not one other race of people can proclaim this level of strength, and for that reason I know we are not only resilient, but are targeted. The original design of the Statue of Liberty was a black woman with chains on her hands and feet as a gift to slaves from France representing that slavery had ended, conversely, the U.S. denied the original design as they wanted to erase any reference to slavery. Still to this day, the Statue of Liberty still have the chains on her legs. Yet, Washington, D.C. and all its beauty was built by slaves, Benjamin Banneker was one of those slaves who designed the layout. He mastered the clocks, he once took the back off a pocket watch to see how it worked and went home and made a clock out of wood with all the gears that it needed to properly communicate the time, the Big Ben is the clock in London, coined after him.

We are fearfully and wonderfully made, the struggle that created this vexed attitude is not who you are, it's what you adapted to. We learned our way of living from broken, dismantled, and hurt people. Our ancestors literally watched their husband beaten within an inch of his life, their child sold, loved ones hung on the 4th of July as it was tradition, and their daughters, themselves, and other women repeatedly raped. In which, the raping was not against the law because there was a law that protected the aggressor. Black women were said to be lustful and promiscuous, in fact wanted the sex. The attitudes we have and the loudness is not wrong, it's just different more of an outwardly cry, it's a result of 400 plus years of trauma without intervention, help, or treatment. What we do when we have the attitude and loudness sometimes is wrong. We are so precious and so unique that they performed experiments on us to see what was in us. Henrietta Lacks, was an African American woman whose cancer cells were the source of the HeLa cell line, the first immortalized cell line and one of the most important cell lines in medical research. Her cells were used to treat individuals who were going blind, cancer, polio, and even an AIDS cocktail. They used her cells in bombs and in outer space. The John Hopkins hospital called the cell HeLa to refrain for using Henrietta Lacks name. J. Marion Sims, whom society named "father of Gynecology" performed many experiments on enslaved women and children. He is famous for the countless experimental operations without the benefit of anesthesia or before any type of antiseptic on women and the shoemaker's awl he used on infants. Benjamin Rush, whom society named the "father of American psychiatry", believed that African Americans bore "negritude". He believed that this was a disease that caused our skin to be dark. Of course, melanin is the cause of our skin being dark, the darker your skin the more melanin you have. Melanin is much more than the pigment of your skin color, that is only the surface, which they (American scientist and doctors) soon found out. Through experiments they found that melanin slows aging and protects from damaging effects of sunlight, the darker the skin the less it ages. They continued to find that melanin increases the speed of nerve and brain messages transmitted between the left and the right hemispheres of the human brain. Scientist specified that the less melanin in an individual, the more calcified the pineal gland and less access the individual has to the spiritual world. They discovered that melanin was the key to life itself, and that Africans possessed more melanin than any other race. We are different, but not inferior. Our views have been altered and manipulated but not destroyed. Our understanding and cognitive behavior has been bleached and brainwashed but not dismantled. We have lost our mothers, children and fathers along our journey, and everything we do wrong the media place a magnifying glass on it, but we'll rise like the sun at dawn.

There are many who believe that we are incompetent, and lack the ability to be great simply because we are women. But I beg to differ, African American Women have the potential to change situations, circumstances, and lives for the betterment of humanity. If you don't agree, let's just take a glimpse into the strength, knowledge, and power of Black Girls.

> ***Elizabeth Freeman***, *one of the most effective abolitionists of the eighteenth century.* ***Phillis Wheatley****, a widely eminent poet, embezzled by slave traders at the age of seven (7) or eight (8).* ***Sojourner Truth, born Isbella Baumfree*** *was sold four (4) times before she ran*

away permanently. Truth went through a conversion that left her the committed activist for all men and women. **Harriet Tubman**, *conceivably the most inspirational of all abolitionists. I live by the very statement she proclaimed, "There was one or two things I had a right to, liberty or death; if I could not have one, I would have the other; for no man should take me alive; I should fight for my liberty as long as my strength lasted, and when the time come for me to go, the Lord would let them take me."* **Ida B. Wells-Barnett**, *she devoted her adult life to a successful anti-lynching campaign. She lost both parents at the age of 16, she became the only provision to her five siblings. She lied about her age to take a job as a teacher, supporting her family on twenty-five dollars a month. She finally found that 1,217 African Americans had been hung between the years of 1890 and 1900. Ida B. Wells-Barnett was a dominant founder of National Association for the Advancement of Colored People (NAACP) in 1909.* **Mary Church Terrell**, *an exceptionally efficacious advocate of women's rights- particularly black women's rights. She was the first African America woman to be appointed to the Washington, D.C., Board of Education in 1895. She aided the National American Woman Suffrage Association in passing the Nineteenth amendment, she was one of the founders of National Association of Colored Women and a founder of NAACP. She also pressured American Association of University Women to open their doors to black women.* **Sarah Breedlove also known as Madame C.J. Walker**, *lost her first husband to a lynch mob at twenty. Destitution and bad nutrition, merged with traditional "wrap and twist" hair straightening methods, made her hair begin to thin. By the time she met her second husband C.J. Walker she and her relatives had already began filling jars with product, he trained her on the marketing and mail order procedures that turned her small business into a million-dollar success.* **Bessie Coleman**, *the first African American female aviator.* **Bessie Smith**, *"Empress of the Blues".* **Zora Neale Hurston**, *one of the celebrated* writers of the Harlem Renaissance. **Marian Anderson**, the best opera singer in the world. **Katherine Dunham**, one of the nation's most prominent choreographers, and an enthusiastic activist for all people of African heritage. **Billie Holiday, born Eleonora Fagan**, was easily one of the most captivating singers of the 1930s, 1940s, and 1950s. Gwendolyn Brooks, the 1949 Pulitzer Prize winning poet. **Ruby Dee**, built what W. Calvin Anderson called a "sober allegiance to a proud African oral tradition and a rich African American folklore." **Fannie Lou Hamer**, a woman who nearly lost her life while trying to register African American voters in the Deep South. **Shirley St. Hill Chisholm** was the first African American woman selected to the U.S. Congress and the first African American to blastoff a campaign for a major party presidential nomination. **Maya Angelou**, the U.S. poet Laureate. **Lorraine Hansberry**, playwright and civil rights activist. **Toni Morrison, born Chloe Anthony Wofford**, grew to be one of the most noteworthy novelists of this age. **Marian Wright Edelman**, keen civil rights activist and founder of the Children's Defense Fund (CDF). **Wilma Rudolph**, who overpowered polio to win three gold medals in the track occurrences at the 1960 Summer Olympics. **Mary McLeod Bethune**, founder of the Daytona Normal and Industrial School. Loyal to education she later combined the coeducational Cookman Institute to form the Buthune-Cookman College. She devoted her time to education and ecivil rights, and precisely that of African American women, Bethune gave a lifetime to the establishment and organization of groups like the powerful National Council of Negro Women (1935) and the National Youth Administration (NYA), which U.S. President Roosevelt requested her to counsel as the Director of Negro Affairs. She was also a member of the National Association of Colored Women (NACW), which she aligned with the primarily white International Council of Women.

This is evidence that we can overcome and achieve all things we set our minds to. Those women rose to the occasion despite the harsh and cruel bold acts of racism and sexism. If they can go after change in a time as such then we should commit to strive and create change for the current issues we face now. As you research the life of these women, you will discover that these women collaborated and formed organizations to create change for African Americans. They were well educated and designed a plan that assisted African American women and children an opportunity to rise. Those women became legendary and left a legacy. What these illustrious women have done supports everything I have told you throughout this book. When you focus on the purpose that God has placed in your life, things that seem impossible are mere road bumps. Things that are questionable turns into I cannot believe I achieved that, and things that people have tried but failed to do becomes your chance to testify. When you walk in your destiny, racism cannot stop you. Bad relationships cannot hold you, and mistakes cannot set you back. When you are walking in your destiny your stronghold is you, only you can slow you down. We must cease with giving people and things the authority over our lives. We find our purpose by spending time with God, and little do we know, majority of the time our purpose is something we love to do the most. Our purpose most times is something we wouldn't have dreamed of getting paid for. Your purpose will never be for you but you will reap the reward for it, so if you are self-serving and all about me, my, mines you are not purpose driven. Our gifts are to give, not to keep. He trusted you with a specific gift that earth needed and once you release it, it will be for the betterment of someone else. I told you before, the Kingdom operates on a one another foundation. Take the time to research the "Greats" and see how many you find focused on finding a man with money, focused on getting money for personal gain, or to show off. You will find that a result of giving, serving, and enhancing others' lives that they reap a harvest.

I was once told that a man is not measured by what that comes to him, but by what goes through him. The richest place in America is the cemetery, there are so many that left here without fulfilling their purpose. I just wonder which one of them held the cure for HIV. I just wonder which one of them held the cure for cancer, and which one held the cure for juvenile diabetes. The cure for these diseases that we cannot seem to master will not come by osmosis, but through an individual. I beg you to encourage our youth, reach out to the brother on the street, and ministry to the poor because we all know that God has no respective person. He used a man who was murdering Christians to restore them, He used a man who collected taxes to reimburse something that was more valuable than money, He used fishermen to hook souls so we know that he will use those that the society look down on as the one the society needs. So, don't get on that high horse to look down, but use it as a tool to extend a helping hand to all our brothers and sisters.

To Be Real Or To Be To Fake

To be real or to be fake,
That is the question.
Rather it is modernistic to face genocide and its offenses
To reject lashes, inches, make-up, and implants
Or accept instance criticism for your naturalistic.
To be real or to be fake,
That is the question.
Because even your attitude change when you wear these things
Trying to be someone in America.
The great country that your ancestors built,
Blood, sweat, and tears over 400 years
And this country still discarding us.
To be real or to be fake,
That is the question.
Reparation being paid to the Indians, Japanese, and to the Jewish people from Germany,
But what happened to you and me? What's the conspiracy?
America, the country that tells you who you should be.
To be real or to be fake,
That is the question.
To be a politician is to be Real Fake!
Giving false dreams, and saying things like let's "Make America Great Again",
Read between the lines, what is it chains or lies
As to why you can't face the Truth!
To be real or to be fake,
That is the question.
Hidden history, secrecy, lies piling like flies on treachery.
America is not for you nor me!
Just to be real!

A'MIA P. WRIGHT

CHAPTER 5
Know Your Worth

"Dreams are to be fulfilled, He gave the dream to the right being"

As a teenager, my grandmother once told me that the world is a force to be reckoned with. She voiced that if you are ignorant to the way the world operates, you will become gullible and believe and do anything. She carried on saying, "you are in high school now. You should know a little bit about everything, and enough about anything so that you can converse with anyone." I hold dear to a lot of things my Grandmother told me because I admired her for all the things I had witnessed her overcome and achieve. Although, I wasn't the best child in the world, she made sure I knew my value and my worth. I strongly believe that a woman's number one thing to have should be self-worth versus attitude. Your attitude is something that can be altered by the right gesture, but it's tough to persuade a girl with self-worth. Her focal point will be of ways in which she can be elevated. We evaluate our relationships like a financial plan. We have to map out the P&L (profit and loss) what will we gain and what will we have to sacrifice for this relationship, cash flow (money management) can he manage his money well enough so that we do not get into the habit of borrowing other people money when we become a family, and balance sheet (pump or dump) could this be a long term relationship or just a fling. It's not so much a money thing, but we understand that we deserve the best, and we strive to do our best. I would never forget the story my grandparents told me of how they met. Of course, they each said that one was more interested in pursuing a relationship than the other, but according to the story they both agreed that my Grandfather would wait in the curve of the street that my Grandmother walked home after school every day in his green convertible mustang with white leather interior. She stated that he would say, "hey Almeria Wilmore" and she'd continue walking, but one day she stopped and talked to him.

A couple days later he came to her house and asked her mother permission to date her. My great grandmother allowed him to date her daughter. She graduated from high school two years later and went on to college at Grambling State University. She said she would come home from college every weekend and he would take her shopping and back to school on Sunday. A few things in this story caught my attention: 1) my grandmother knew her value 2) my grandfather was very consistent 3) my grandfather valued my grandmother and respected her mother enough to ask her permission. Through my grandfather, I witnessed that a man makes many mistakes but it's the way he cleans them up that determines whether you should continue to build with him. Through my Grandmother I witnessed that sometimes even the strongest woman has to fight pride and continue to love her man even when it seems impossible to recover your love. Their marriage has been 46 years strong, and they grow closer every year. It's funny how they mirror each other so perfectly. Their marriage is the epitome of what God has bound together, let no man tear apart. Her self-worth and his ability to value her and to be consistent transitioned into many years together.

How to build self-worth?

The first step to building self-worth is to accept and love yourself the way God loves and accepts you, as you are, period! A lot of women may say, "oh I love me some me." If that is so, why are you allowing yourself to be used? Why do you need the approval of Facebook frenemies to determine if you are beautiful, popular, or right or wrong? When you truly love, and accept yourself, you have a clear and concise understanding of who you are and whose you are. You know without a doubt that you are not a piece of property, sex tool, or baby making machine. You believe wholeheartedly that the God you serve loves you so much that He knows the number of hairs on your head. He set provisions for you before you entered the womb. He placed a purpose in you that earth needed. When you love, and accept yourself, you will understand that true identity is found in Christ and any other identity will self-destruct. We will realize that the continuous use of make-up accelerates our aging. It is perfectly fine to wear but when we wear it to cover up who we are then it becomes harmful. We will have to understand that excessive weight can destroy us physically. Today women are gaining excessive weight only to hear that we are "thick". Most of African American Women gain weight in the abdominal area, hips, thighs, and buttocks. The weight leads to heart problems, diabetes, high cholesterol, obesity and many other health issues that shorten our lives and limits our ability to live. We must understand that our health is so precious that God voiced that above all things he wishes that we prosper and be in good health as our souls shall prosper, 3 John 2:1. If health wasn't important, He wouldn't have mentioned it. Good health creates an opportunity for longevity. So, if these two falsified identities are self-destructive, why do we encourage this? We must spend time with our designer to understand the uniqueness he bestowed upon each one of us. There is nothing about us that is a coincidence. Every mole, permanent scar, and freckle was placed exactly where He designed it to go. Then he turned around and gave each one of us something that will tell us apart that cannot be copied. He gave us fingerprints. There are no two people of the 6 billion plus people on earth that have the same fingerprints, not even twins.

That was His way of saying that you are the same but you are all different. Love yourself the way God loves you.

The second step of building self-worth is to have discipline. Discipline is having the ability to maintain structure and self-control. The lack of discipline is a path of hardships and mistakes that very well could be avoided if you have discipline. When you are disciplined it protects your self-worth because your conscious reminds you why or why not the decision you are struggling with is for you. Discipline prepares you for opportunities that others miss out on. I had a co-worker that was hired a little bit after me. She started off good, but then a couple more girls were hired and they became friends. The girls hired after her were very irresponsible and lacked discipline. They continuously showed up to work late and it began to influence her. So, one day the girls began to talk recklessly about the immediate supervisor via monitored emails after being warned and having knowledge of the monitoring. The lack of self-discipline landed all the girls on the unemployment list. She was not disciplined enough to separate herself from mischief. It caused her to lose her job. Discipline teaches respect for others and respect for self. Discipline will teach us how to dress, how to cover our assets in public, and how to keep our legs together until we feel he is worthy of our goods. Discipline protects us from conceiving multiple children with multiple men and neither one of them providing for their children. Discipline protects us from making a living off government assistance. Discipline causes us to hold our head high and puff out our chest. Discipline restricts us from social media drama and exposed pages. Discipline protects us from ourselves, because as I've said, our worst enemy is us. As you journey through life setting goals to reach, it is discipline that will keep you aligned with what you have set out to do. It is discipline that protects your dreams, and prepares you to face opposition. Ladies, get you some discipline.

The third step of building self-worth is to have integrity. Integrity is doing what is right when no one is around, it is being morally sound. Many people lack integrity, especially at the work place. Integrity is a characteristic that is very important, it can be the determining factor in that promotion you had your eye on. It can be the determining factor in a decision the bank makes on the mortgage loan for that new home you want for your family. It can even be a determining factor for the neighborhood you live in. Integrity creates a great reputation for you, as it is said that your reputation is like your credit score once it's bad it is hard to restore it. Your reputation follows you everywhere you go, and affects all that you seek to accomplish. Integrity will protect you from a criminal background, such as theft, sexual offender, or robbery. Integrity will weigh your options before you make a decision that could alter your life negatively. Many organizations instruct their members to have integrity to protect their organization from having a bad reputation such as, the military, NBA, NFL, NHL, MLB, and most Fortune 500 companies just to name a few. God will not promote us unless we have the right character for that promotion. Ladies, integrity is a very special ingredient to build self-worth.

The Word says that we should be quick to listen and slow to speak. We must control our tongues, for it has the power to hurt as well as heal and restore. We cannot allow our emotions to speak for us because emotions change like Louisiana weather. If you have ever lived in Louisiana you know that one minutes it's storming, one minute the sun is bright, the next minute it's snowing, hypothetically speaking. The weather is unstable and inconsistent; such is our emotions. One minute we can feel happy, sad, overwhelmed, and every other emotion but the minute something wanted happens the emotions changes to fit the situation. But a woman of love and acceptance, a woman of discipline, and a woman of integrity can tame her tongue. She may think it but we keep it zipped up. We overlook a lot of petty things that may cause us harm. We respond to negativity with pleasure and well thought out words, we refuse to react out of emotion. Self-worth is founded upon these things, ladies let's build self-worth and demolish those negative statistics that the world placed on us as being ghetto, loud, obnoxious, and disrespectful. The key to success is simple. It's goals. A millionaire is a millionaire because he/she set a goal and went above and beyond to obtain each one.

Just or Unjust

Strange fruit Billie Holiday that was the truth
Dropped from the trees like rotten apples do.
They threw away the nooses and grabbed a round or two
Put on uniforms and badges
But it's the same heart issue.
It's a crime to be Black
And we can't escape that truth.
The melanin in our skin only gets darker with sunlight
Sometimes the future doesn't seem so bright.
From hanging from trees
To lying face down on concrete
Nothing has changed since your sweet melodies.
We are still facing danger
Because of this skin disease
That's the lie they hoped we'd believe
Same way they sold the dream
That it was a disease to want to be freed.
Head on a swivel running with wings
Us against the world
Is the way it seems
Still lashing from backlashes
Massa put on Madea in the past
It's so hard to laugh
When living life under a magnifying glass
Guns trained to blast
Before questions are asked
The bigger the man
The faster the heartbeat
Finger on the trigger so tight when he tweak
We sleep on to eternal destiny
While he takes a paid vacation with his family
God's justice got to be sweet
This can't be the path He choose for thee!

CHAPTER 6
Fairness, For Whom?

"All We Know is Pain and Work"

In the 1800's President Lincoln set his sights on the future for the United States. He saw that the civil war could not reunite the South and the North into a union again and it would destroy the country all together. He realized that the South had an economic advantage over the North due to slavery. The South was growing too powerful and capitalism began to rise, and the North understood that the enslavement of African people was stifling capitalism. The North noticed that they would have over production and no one to buy, but the South could sell its raw materials all over the world. So, Honest Ab, as they called him, decided to sign off on the Emancipation Proclamation and force the South to free their slaves. Lincoln stated, "there is a physical difference between the white and the black races which I believe will forever forbid the two races living together…while they do remain together there must be the position of superior and inferior, and I as much as any man am in favor of having the superior position assigned to the white race (Browder, 1992, p.18)." After he "freed" the slaves in the South, we begin to migrant North. Some Northern states were preventing slaves from entering by threatening to give them 39 lashes and imprisonment, Oregon was one of the states that denied slaves entrance. They set us free and told us to pull ourselves up by our boot straps. They denied us jobs so we had no means to provide which lead us to returning to the original slave owner for work. The original slave owner then loan the ex-slave the equipment to work at an alarming rate that he/she could not afford which resulted in him working seven years for no pay, which is still slavery.

The government then created ghettos for blacks, the first record of ghettos was in Europe not Africa or America. The government then set up a system that restricted, handicapped, and hung Blacks called welfare and child support. Once blacks dependent on this system, they began to utter, "they always want something for free". It's very ironic because the "Headright System" - was created by the government and the purpose of this system was to bring more Europeans to America, they were told that if they came to America the government would give 160 acres of land to the head of household. If they brought indentured servants or slaves over with them then they will be given an additional 50 to 100 acres for each slave or indentured servant all for FREE", but we must pull ourselves up by our boot straps. Later, there was the "Homestead Act of 1862" - this was also given by the government, this Act gave land to Whites only. It was after this Act that Lincoln signed the Emancipation, there was no mention of reparation to blacks, but 930 slave owners partitioned the government for reparation for releasing the slaves. They were paid $300 per slave by the government. But we had to pull ourselves up by our boot straps. Then, there was the "Redlining and VA Loans of the 1930's-1960's, this Act is where the FHA stepped in and started giving low interest loans to white vets only for homes. The redlining was a map used to ensure that the vets did not get placed in the Black neighborhoods. Blacks were not approved for these loans. But we are the ones always looking for something free? Everything we have including the breath we take, we had to fight, work, and suffer for. Nothing was given to us but lies and pain. When we began to pull ourselves up by our boot straps, Black Wall Street for example, it was destroyed because we were coming up too fast. When we mention the lack of jobs and Black owned businesses, they mention affirmative action. Affirmative action was not created for Blacks. It was created for white women. White women are the biggest recipients of the affirmative action act not Blacks. Henry Berry, Virginia House of Representatives: "We have, as far as possible, closed every avenue by which the light may enter the slave's mind. If we could extinguish the capacity to see the light, our work will be complete. They would then be on the level of the beast of the fields, and we then should be safe." I understand so clearly what James Baldwin stated, "To be a Negro in this country and to be relatively conscious is to be in a rage almost all the time."

I've noticed that when other races speak about their homeland and the history of their homeland, it is noted as being patriated. But when Blacks discuss their history and homeland, we are coined militant, Afrocentric, or rebels. The stories taught in history classes are fabricated, filled with add-ons, subtractions, and painted faces. It's not 100% pure, my mother always told me if it's a little lie in the story, it's a lot of lie in the author, don't trust any of it. The biggest lie ever told is, "sticks and stones may break my bones but words will never hurt me." Words were used to shape and form the world, words are used to declare war, and words are used to outwardly express how you feel about someone or something. I can only imagine why our ancestors began to say and believe this. Then, I asked myself, if the world as you know it was against you, would you fold or would you find a way to stand firm? As for me, I would have without a doubt guarded my heart and buried my feelings. That saying was an outwardly expression that although words have the ability destroy, we also can reject the allowance of your words into our hearts. There were many derogatory statements were made about blacks, these statements flowed from the mouths of regular citizens as well as Presidents. Thomas Jefferson in "Notes on the State of Virginia" (1787) stated that he personally thought that black men preferred white women over their own. This ASSumption lead to those who were incapable of thinking for themselves, and had the inability to learn the truth the opportunity to become more fearful. That fear amplified in white women who would scream rape if a black man even looked at her. He totally disregarded that the highest percentage of interracial children stemmed from a black woman being raped by a white man. He also preferred black women, please make note that he had children with Sally Hemings, a slave woman on his plantation. We had to force ourselves to live in an imaginary world to withstand the cruel and harsh reality we were facing. We had to steal a smile from a lie, and take laughter from a cry. Our ancestors came into this world being trained to fear white people, respect white people, and submit to white people. Whites come into this world being trained to maintain power and that they are superior to all races. There is one thing that white people are naturally afraid of, and that's black people. I once heard a white man that had recently converted from racism say, "we are afraid of blacks because we are afraid of having what was done to them, done to us." Blacks are not individualized as whites are when a crime is committed. For instances, if a black man commits a crime, it's immediately directed to the whole race, "that's just the way they are". But if a white man commits a crime, he committed the crime on his own, "he has psychologically issues" as it cannot be directed to the whole race.

Again, I say, pull yourselves up by your boot straps women. The road we tread has not been fair, and there have been many advantages given to other races but we must continue to dig and pull. Everything that was accomplished by our ancestors was conquered in unity, support, and dedication. When Harriet Tubman began to lead slaves to freedom she carried a shotgun, not for the bounty hunters but for those slaves who wanted to turn and go back. We cannot escape or avoid talking about racism. It may be awkward and uncomfortable, but white supremacy must be addressed. Racism is a global system for the genetic survival of the global white minority population. Racism is a very touchy topic, it's very painful to discuss but nevertheless, it must be reviewed. Blacks are automatically expecting whites to be empathic and sorrowful, on the other hand whites are automatically thinking we weren't the ones who enslaved your ancestor's, the battlefield is now level so quit expecting us to apologize for the past and get on with life. Both viewpoints are wrong, blacks should not expect anything from anyone but our own people. We must help each other heal. Whites should not think that by what happened during slavery it does not affect them, the ground is level, or that years of trauma without an intervention just disappears because it does not. Whites still benefit from slavery, the playing field is more uneven than it was doing slavery, and any scar that is not properly cared for becomes infected. Racism is real and visible, too visible to say it's 2017 but it is very clear that hate does not die. I am not assuming the entire race of people are racist, that's irrational thinking. That is very naïve and closed minded. That's as preposterous as saying racism does not exist at all. But that is the elephant in the room that we all need to properly address to progress. The reason this subject is constantly being swept under the rug is because those who are in power are not affected, it's only "you people" that have a problem and "you people" are invisible. I remember one time in the grocery store, I was walking in the produce area and a white young adult age range female was walking towards me, her side had a corner so she had to cross in front of me to get through. I kid you not, this rude, ill-mannered, and disrespectful young adult walked towards me and if I would not have stepped over she would have run into me but she never apologized or said excuse me. The flesh side of me wanted to knock her shoulder off but I have too much to lose and a mission to accomplish. I was taught to choose your battles, that could have easily turned bad and landed "me" in jail and in the newspaper and messed up everything I busted my buttocks for. But how can you respect or include someone that is not even considered human, but is only 3/5ths a person? That would require revamping the Constitution which should have been the first thing to change if we were "set free" but that was a political decision it had nothing to do with slaves. It would require the laws changing, and the mindsets changing of those who see blacks as untamed beast of the field because the country was set up for us to forever be slaves. How is that freedom? In what ways does Blacks suffer from racism? Economically, blacks are the most unemployed race of people in America. In March of 2017, the unemployment rate for Blacks was

22.9 percent, and although whites triple us their unemployment rate was only 14.0 percent. Housing, blacks are placed in ghettos, slums and section 8 housing in a particular area of the town that is very far from the whites. In these areas the conditions are poor, unmaintained, and unsafe but if you can't afford better even though you may not be interested in drugs, violence, and crime you are forced to reside in these areas because it all you can afford. It does not matter how good your heart is, a sheep cannot survive in a cage of wolves. You will either become a wolf or suffer as a sheep. Thus, the children in these areas have no choice but to become a wolf to avoid constant teasing and picking from peers or being prey to some pervert. History has proven that blacks are a race of people that adapt to their environment to make it suitable for them to live. Education, blacks suffer deeply in this area because most schools in urban neighborhoods are neglected. We are stuck between a rock and a wall when it comes to education. Those of us who pursue education are burned by the student loans, by the time we graduate we're buried with debt. We start our career digging ourselves out of at least $50,000 of student loans, and what's so humorous about this situation is now banks count your student loans against you when you are trying to purchase a home. Our parents were not able to pay for our education, in fact, most of our parents live paycheck to paycheck. They are "Just Over Broke", so education is important but making sure your sisters and brothers have shelter and food is a little more important. On the flip side, there are blacks who refuse to follow the mouse trap and choose not to go to college, not understanding that today a piece of paper is worth more than a skill because they have to weed us out in order to keep their own. To compete in America a degree is the starting point. Count it a blessing to thrive without one if you are black. Healthcare, this topic leads to many questions, especially now that it is required and affect your taxes. If my month has always been longer than my money, or I am barely making ends meet, why would I add another bill to myself? How can I afford healthcare? If I make too much to acquire Medicaid, but too little to allow Cigna, Aetna, United Healthcare, or any other medical insurance agency deduct $75 and up from my paycheck every time I'm paid or monthly $100 plus. What do we do? Those individuals who possess Medicaid most times have doctors who perform very little research to properly aid their patients, and often experiment to see which drug help the patient. It's trial and error because it's a charity hospital. The main reason the rich declined Obamacare, they refused to allow poor people to use the same doctor as they do. Again, blacks are strongly affected. For all the reasons I just mentioned, racism and white supremacy needs to be addressed. Believe it or not, many blacks have no idea what racism or white supremacy is or what it looks like when it's encountered.

The media only makes it worst, when they discover a story they find someone that has chosen many hard paths in life to represent us worldwide. Propaganda is a fool. The media have the whole U.S.A thinking we are a bunch of low life, uneducated, illiterate fools and it's our people that laugh and repost the videos. Fool, this reflects you too, this is how they see us all. To them it's only a handful of blacks that are civil, intelligent, and classy, and they are labeled "uppity" blacks. I understand Marshawn Lynch reasoning for refusing to talk to the media, but society labeled him a thug, a militant, and uncooperative. He planned and implemented. He conquered what he set out to do. I don't know about anywhere else in the world but in Louisiana, thugs do not build schools, and they most definitely not looking to improve the youth lives. Thugs have one mindset, live reckless and die young. Be careful what you allow the media to impose on you. Racism affects our everyday lives because the system was created for us to fail. All the laws that were passed by ALEC (American Legislative Exchange Council), for instance, the 3 strikes law that they urged former President Bill Clinton to bring about (that he later apologized for) and like-minded individuals that think you are scum of the earth are still in effect. ALEC is a private sector that create laws based on economics, education, and other common denominators then urge the lawmakers to make it a law. ALEC collaborate with the CCA (Corrections Corporation of America) who makes billions from massive incarceration, to keep the prisons filled. The Constitution still today label us as 3/5ths a man, which means we are not even human, just property. These old slavery and chain gang laws still exist but we worried about beefing on Facebook, Twitter, Instagram, and SnapChat. We are blind to the fact that they are plotting on continuously filling the prisons with our children. They are continuously slaughtering our men, and we as women have been sold as a penny with a hole in it to the entire world. At the rate we are going, we will be the first race to repeat physical slavery. The modern-day plantations are so over populated that they are releasing men and women with lesser crimes to make room, and you are a plum fool if you think for one second that they are releasing us. Slavery never ended, they just removed the chains and gave you a television. Every time you turn on the "show box" as my great grandmother called it, you are being reminded that you are inferior, a wild untamed beast, thug, drug head, prostitute, drug dealer, pathetic and needy. In other words, they are drilling in your head that you are incompetent and inhumane, therefore you belong in a cage under close watch and instructions.

Drapetomania was a conjectural mental illness that, in 1851, "American physician" Samuel A. Cartwright hypothesized to cause Black slaves to flee captivity. This guy was coined "American physician" for making up a disease that he thought encouraged slaves to want to be free. This is the place where you scream "Oh My Goodness" also known as "OMG". When you research the foundation of these modern-day father of individuals you discover that they are lies, experiments, or mere opinions they shared, absolutely none of it was true. Which further leads me to believe that bigotries and racist base their hate on pure assumption. As great and as important as African American history is to American history, it is totally undermining that it cannot and is not included in the history books. Uncovering our history requires revealing the truth about America's founding fathers. It would require rewriting these textbooks that we aren't mentioned in. Releasing our history is irrelevant because the elusion they have deceived people into believing will awaken people and display the truth of how we lived, how we died, and how America took our inventions and originations as their own. I must pose a few questions only because the fact that Blacks live, breathe, and function properly it was a type of disease or experiment that had to be performed. We need an intervention to heal this pain, this hurt, this anger but so does whites. They need to heal from the hatred, the jealousy, and the fear. So, what is the disease that cause people to hate because of the color of another race skin? What is the disease that cause people to enslave a race of people for over 400 years? What is the disease that cause these cops to murder so many people? What is the disease that cause people to think that they are superior to another race of people? What is the disease that cause the media to belittle a race of people? What is the disease that causes propaganda? And I can go on forever, but my point is those questions would lead more to a disease than the color of someone skin, slaves wanting to be freed, and all other foolishness these men have the world bamboozled by. God created all races. What is the disease that caused man to dysfunction the assembly that God crafted? What amazes me about the black race is, we have so many reasons to be "off the hinges", totally bananas, I mean so mentally dysfunctional that no one could explain but we are so far from mentally ill. In fact, we are so mentally sane that we still manage to conquer and achieve goals, we are still able to capture the level of normalcy that America set as their own, and we still rise despite it all. That alone assures me that God is real and living.

Eventuality
"For every voice that said no you can't, there is a greater voice that is saying yes you can!"

If you have found yourself in some of the situations that are mentioned it this book, understand that this is not to belittle you or hurt you. Please understand that I wrote this book because I strongly believe in us as women and I believe in us as a culture. In life there are obstacles, oppositions, and setbacks but every day you open your eyes you have an opportunity to change your life. Every day is a new beginning for someone who has endured enough, to shake the excuses and fears and live life. Greatness is within each one of us, but it will not uproot itself nor will it enhance itself without you. Earl Nightingale once said, "people with goals succeed because they know where they are going." It is never too late to chase your dream, after all, it's your dream and you are responsible for making it a reality. Within this book, I have expressed how we have allowed ourselves to be seen. I have shined light on how we are treated by our men, how to migrate towards greatness, how we should honor those before us, and how to establish self-worth to leave a legacy for those after us. Let's take heed and break the cycle of fatherless children; break the cycle of allowing men to degrade us; break the cycle of burying our youth and young adults to violence, and break the cycle of our children in and out of prison. Some people say reach for the stars, then there are some that say reach for the moon, and even if you miss you will still be amongst the stars. I say reach for God for He is the only One reaching back and if you fail you will still come out VICTORIOUS! To God you are as precious as the most valuable jewel on this earth. You are His very own child, and His portal to deliver what earth needs to earth. You are so special that He compares you to His Church. No excuses needed. Be the Queen He created you to be. Have you ever witnessed a chained dog that desperately wanted to get loose, especially after seeing another animal? Well, such is your soul when its bound by the things of this world that mean you no good. Your soul knows its rightful place, and all other places will be unsettling. The most significant thing I noticed about the women I mentioned in chapter four is that all of them knew that it was impossible to change history, present and future without education. If you were to advance you would need education to protest for equal rights, jobs, and to vote. Voting is another topic for another book, but I must say that we have Blacks in great numbers refusing to vote because they figure our vote do not count. This to me is true in a sense that the 3/5th clause or 3/5 Compromise is still in effect. The 3/5th a person clause came into effect because Congress was split into two different groups, which are Senates and House of Representatives. The number of Senates you get in the House of Represents is based on your population, how many people reside in that State. Because of this the South wanted to know if they could count the slaves as a part of the population to increase the chances of controlling the House. However, slaves were not considered citizens and the North reminded the South that the slaves were not even consider human but property, therefore they did not count. The South demanded to include the slaves because they wanted to insert more Representatives in Congress which would mean more power. After a great debate amongst the founding fathers they came up with a comprise. They decided to count the slaves as 3/5ths a person. For example, three white people vote equaled 5 votes but only 3 votes out of 5 slaves would count. Because the Constitution has not changed every time there is an election and you see the South painted red, you should be reminded of the Constitution and what it thinks of you. So, we must push harder to equal out when it comes to voting in the South, although slavery was everywhere. The South benefited more and the long-term influence of slavery made the South slave owners more disturbed than those in the North. We allow our own to deceive us into not voting, then we are the first to cry out about injustice because we are the ones who receives the harshest ends of all the back-door arrangements Congress allows to pass. At least vote someone into office that will give you a chance, verses not voting and allowing the ones in office who will allow the officers to gun you down in the street and get a paid vacation. We should learn to think logically and with reasoning, we cannot allow someone else selfish reasons prevent us from making progress. Through voting there are laws passed, and most times not to your benefit. Back when the law for "war on drugs" was first passed by Richard Nixon it was a political move for the people, the actual "war on drugs" movement began with Ronald Reagan. He really began stuffing the prisons with so many African American men. Meanwhile, they started implementing laws and amendments that affected blacks. Because those people who were voting could not read well, bribery was used to pass laws that aimed for African American youth and young adults.

Dr. Joy DeGury, a nationally and internationally renowned researcher, educator, author and presenter. She is the author of Post Traumatic Slave Syndrome. She shined a light on Thomas Jefferson speech at the end of his term. Her discovery revealed a couple of things to me. One that although Jefferson owned hundreds of slaves, ultimately, he knew that it was wrong. Secondly, Thomas knew that his people were sick for what they did and continuously do to blacks. She stated that Thomas Jefferson was fully aware of what the long-term impact of enslavement on white people and black people would be. Jefferson spoke about the horror associated with what the slave master did and that their children would imitate it amongst their friends and other children who were enslaved. Dr. Joy stated that Thomas Jefferson's greatest fear was that it would end in an extermination in one or the other race. Thomas Jefferson said, "God cannot side with us in this contest. He cannot side with us, which means He(God) will side with them. I tremble when I think about the future of my country as I consider that God is just and that His justice cannot sleep forever." Thomas Jefferson at some point in his life began to realize that the cruelty, mistreatment, and pain that they inflicted upon Blacks was an offense that would one day require justice. Although he was said to be an atheist, at some he realized God justice will prevail much and it would not be in his favor. If you step to the plate everyday with the right mindset, one of these days you will hit a flying drive center field. But you cannot even strike out if you are too afraid to get in the ball game. Women, how can we fix this mistake? I believe in our people. I believe in those who see us as people, and help us to fight against injustice. I believe that we can unite and grow as one if we restore, rebuild, and replenish a destroyed and dismantled relationship in our community then extend a hand to our brothers and sisters of other nationalities. We cannot help them as we are patched together, and they cannot free us from this horror movie but standing up for us in times of injustice gives us a sense of hope and a sense of belonging. Women, we must organize and structure programs that uplift our youth and young adults and increases togetherness. I always wanted to be athlete and real estate investor growing up, but as I began the journey of I said to myself, why don't you try to become a millionaire? Not for the millions, but the mind of a millionaire is limitless. The knowledge you must entail to become a millionaire sets you apart but it also sets you up to change the world. Apart from my mother's perfect health through the Father of Abraham, Isaac and Jacob, I want togetherness for my people and not just Black people, my people by way of the Body of Christ.

One thing about us as a people, we are a very forgiving people. We've been through a lot and we are still enduring hatred because we are melanated people, nonetheless, we are not bitter about the past. We are not revengeful as a people. We forgive, and we live with the hurt, shame, and pain. Although, there are a lot of racism in America still, there are a lot of good loving kind hearted white people also. Lastly, women, we have to pray for our Black men. We have to pray that they are protected, guided, and given wisdom from the Most High to properly lead us. We have some powerful Black men, but more than normal we have men who refuse to grow up and be a man. The songwriter said it best, when a man loves a woman, he will spend his last dime to get what you need. When a man loves a woman, trust me you'll know. Your worth will be his value. Your worth is what puts the "S" on his chest. Ladies, we have the power and influence to change our future and the future of our children. Let's be GREAT! In closing, as the late great James Brown song, "this is a man's world but it would be NOTHING, NOTHING without a woman or a girl."

Bonus

Welcome to the bonus! If you are overwhelmed with the changes that are much needed within our culture, I challenge you to push through this bonus to be rejuvenated. It would be total hypocrisy if I pressed the issue for change, unity, and forwardness as a culture and never released any solutions to start the foundation. I must admit, I made many of the mistakes I speak about in this book because I wanted to be lazy and allow life to flow as is. By the time I decided to be intentional, I was heading into my sophomore year of college. Thanks to my mother's husband, I had an opportunity to attend a Dave Ramsey seminar at Temple Baptist Church for 13 weeks. Of course, I was the youngest in the class and had no debt except my student loans. Within 13 weeks I had grasped more information about finances than my parents and grandparents. I began to become familiar with my credit score and how it was a representation of me to creditor's. I learned that bankruptcy should be the absolutely last result, that you must make sacrifices and pay your debt off. I fell in love with knowledge and began to read at least 3 to 4 books a day. I would sit in Books-a-Million and Barnes & Noble for hours reading. Rich Dad, Poor Dad was the first finance book I read. But I couldn't connect with him, however, there was an instant connection when I read Dave Ramsey books and attended the seminar. I researched everything I read. Be cautions, just because it's in a book does not mean that it is true. So, I researched for truths and to decipher if his methods fit me. Always study the information you receive to enhance your understanding, but also to know that you know that you know it is the truth. It's not to insult anyone, but it's lazy and naïve to believe what someone tell you without checking the information. Research, research, and research again to build confidence, then put your experiences, your personality, your accountability, your responsibility and your lifestyle in the equation. They will affect the outcome, so be mindful and be intentional.

ECONOMICS

The first topic I will address in the direction of building a solid foundation is economics. Everybody aim to be wealthy but very few are wealthy. I cannot give you an insight on wealth because I have never been wealthy, but I can give you a foundation and a staircase to build stability and to become financially savvy. When I say economics, I am referring to your financial considerations. The first level of foundation is a budget. Budgeting reflects your money management skills, when you apply for a loan they consider your credit score because it informs the creditors of your accountability as it relates to finances. 1. If I loan this person money, can he/she pay it back? 2. Has he/she been in the negative often? 3. Will we have to hassle him/her or send this into collections? Money management is boring I agree, I'd much rather do something a bit more exciting, however, this is a task that cannot be ignored. A budget does not necessarily save you money but it tells you where your money goes. I don't know about you all, but there were so many times I checked my bank account and was dumb faced like what did I spend $300 dollars on in a matter of 2 days? Below is a sample of a basic budget my grandparents started me off with.

Income		Expenses		
Check#1	$600	Food	$200	
Check#2	$600	Rent	$300	
		Insurance	$90	
		Utilities	$130	
		Entertainment	$200	
		Gas	$60	
		Tithe	$120	
Total	$1200		$1100	+$100

This basic budget I prepared is based on a biweekly income of $600. Because I spent my money on paper, I already know automatically I have $100 dollars left after I pay my bills. Most people call this "money to blow" but I call this money to save. Now, I know that if I stick to my budget I can save $100 a month. Not only that, if I decide not to use all $200 dollars on entertainment and only use $75 dollars on entertainment I can save an additional $125 dollars, which means I am now saving $225 a month. Doing that for 6 months becomes $1350 which can buy you 3 to 4 properties, stay tuned and I will tell you how.

Now, that you have your budget set in stone, do not deter from it. In fact, set a reminder to revisit your budget a least twice a month. We have $1300 plus dollars by having discipline and so we want to reward ourselves with shopping, dining in at a restaurant, and/ have a few drinks with friends. As an entrepreneur, I have had first-hand experiences of being passed up by my own people when it comes to products, goods and services. This is because of the broken relationships in our communities. The old mom and pops store use to throb, however, jealousy, lies, and hatred robbed us of that and broke our relationship so much that when we buy from our own people we won't a discount or we don't go back and encourage others to stop going, but we go spend our money in our communities where we are treated poorly, when one of us is murdered they are silent, all they want is your money. We choose them because we are still seeking acceptance, we want to be accepted and visible but the only thing that is visible about you leaves your hand before you leave their store and you pay full price with no debating about a discount. They now money has power, we the only ones that see money to buy things to get a status. But the money is the status. You want to be visible, save your money, spend it in our neighborhoods, and support your own. We allow our people businesses to fail because we refuse to support them. It's lonely at the top because the ones at the top fear sharing the information and going broke again. It is one thing to be broke, but it's a different feeling to be broke, come up, and return to the financial struggle. But ultimately, when you build a brand with zeal, heart, and passion it copyrights itself. No one will be able to clone it. It will be a watered-down version. I had a mentor when I began my nonprofit, Dr. Obadiah Simmons, Jr., very intelligent well rounded man. He taught me to write grants and find funding for my nonprofit. He taught me how to word play because writing grants and being awarded grants all dealt with the proper verbiage. He taught me a solid foundation, and no matter how good I became at writing grants, he was better. My proposals were a watered-down sample of his. While looking for funding, I ran across Ms. Tana Trichel, CEO of Northeast Louisiana Economic Alliance, she fell in love with my hard work so much so that she wanted to hire me. I presented my proposal to her to ask for funding and she admired how structured my writing was, however, when I mentioned who my advisor was, she stated, "He is a very intelligent man, you have an awesome mentor and outstanding grant writer leading you. Be sure to tell him I said hi." His gift was not my gift and he knew that, so he was not afraid to plant a seed. We should train each other in the way we must go to ensure that we are all on the right path.

It will take some time but a little progress is better than being stagnate. Now, I want to inform you of a few things that affect your credit score. There is no need in saving money if you cannot max out every dollar. Your credit score is a tool that banks, dealerships, and many other companies use to decide how much interest you will pay, or APR rate. The higher you credit score the lower the rate and the cheaper the payments, and ultimately, you pay less for that purchase. However, if you have a low credit score than the interest rates are much higher, the payments are much higher, and usually something negative happens like a repo, foreclosure, etc. No credit is just like bad credit when you are trying to purchase essentials like homes and vehicles. How does a credit card affect my credit? A lot of people, even bankers will tell you to get a credit card to build your credit. On the flip side, they forgot to mention that if you spend over 75% of your credit line it affects your score negatively. If you pay it off to fast it affects your score negatively, and if you close your account it affects your score negatively. If you are not disciplined and knowledgeable about credit cards please stay away. What about a loan or line of credit? These are good if you can keep from missing a payment, yet, for every $500 dollars it is only 100 points you build towards your credit. What if I shopped around for a car or house and allowed them to run my credit? Every time someone runs your credit it is believed to take 10 points off your credit score. I am not exactly sure if it is 10 but I know for exact that you do lose points. Can hard inquires be removed? Absolutely, hard inquires just like collections can be removed from your credit report. You can get one free credit report from www.annualcreditreport.com. Collection agencies are third party entities that you are hassled by but you are in no debt to them. I repeat! You do not owe collection agencies a penny. Collection agencies buy your debt for 25% of what it's worth with the intentions to get the other 75% from you. If you've ever spoken with a collection agency they will bargain with you and try to get you to pay at least 75% of the debt. Conversely, the company you actually owe wrote the remaining 75% off as an insurance claim and get their money back plus the 25% that the collection agency pays for your debt. Rule of thumb, never talk to collection agencies. Bust your butt to contact the finance department of the company you owe and pay them. It is a lot of tedious things that affect your credit score such as late payments, closed accounts, collections and etcetera. For instance, you have a payment due but you are a little short this month for whatever reason. If you can, it is perfectly legal to send in as little as $5 a month and that $5 helps you avoid a late payment and it helps you avoid that being reported on your credit score. A good way to build your credit is to get a Certificate of Deposit (CD) and borrow against it, this will allow you to make monthly payments. If you get a credit card, try to keep the usage under 30%, never spend over 75%, if life happens and you must max your card, be conscious of your APR and how much you will have to pay in interest. If the interest rate is too high, research balance transfers and you can transfer your debt to your bank to avoid the interest. Stop! Cosigning for family and friends, they need a cosigner because they are not responsible enough to protect their own credit so now they want to destroy your credit too. Stop getting additional credit cards to pay for the credit card you just maxed, you just created another bill.

Your credit score takes a lot of work, yet, it must be done. As for bankruptcy, bankruptcy is a sign to mortgagor, loan officer, and banks that I have no self-control, I've purchased all this stuff irresponsibly now I cannot pay for it. There are two kinds of bankruptcy, chapter 7 and chapter 13. Chapter 13 bankruptcy occurs when the debtor make enough money to make monthly payments. The discharge is usually take three to five years or completion of payments whichever is first. Chapter 7 bankruptcy is for debtors with low to no income with credit card and medical debt. The discharge is usually three to five months. Chapter 7 bankruptcy is liquidation meaning they can sell your assets to get the money. Chapter 13 allows you to make payments to catch up and dissolve your debt. Chapter 13 bankruptcy was abused a lot until many Blacks started to catch on and do the same thing. It would be used after the debtor attained a big beautiful house, nice luxury vehicle, furnished the house, and toy (boat, 4-wheeler, and/or sports car). Because it had to be reported publicly, my grandmother and I would look in that section every Sunday morning. I understand life happens, but be sure to exhaust all your options before filing bankruptcy.

HOUSING

This is a very interesting section; I mentor a lot of people in this area as it relates to becoming a real estate investor. Buying a home is a very scary thing. To dedicate 15 to 30 years to a loan not knowing what the future holds for you can be devastating. However, there are plenty ways around using a bank and getting drained in high interest rates because of your credit. If you prefer going through a bank because you feel more comfortable and have a good relationship with your banking family that is fine also. Remember to pay at least 20% to avoid the PMI (private mortgage interest) rates that causes your mortgage to fluctuate. Shopping around is good if you cannot afford the 20% because some lenders can and will waive the PMI for you. If you decide to get a realtor make sure that you are comfortable with him/her because you do have the option of getting another realtor at any time. You should find a realtor that has your best interest at heart, and is not just trying to make a sell. Realtors can cover a down payment for you and/or closing cost, be sure to ask about both to see if they will help you out. A lot of people are looking to buy properties to rent them out, however, if you are not a realtor in the state of Louisiana you must wait at least a year before you can rent it out, special circumstances may allow you to rent it out sooner. Be intentional when you decide to buy a home because that is a 15 to 30-year commitment, so visit your state policies and procedures, communicate with a mortgage officer at your bank, and research everything they tell you for your own assurance.

Sometimes taking risks make things uncomfortable but taking risks sometimes benefit us more than being comfortable. The best advice I can give anyone that is signing their name on any piece of paper is to read every word, if you do not understand a word or statement ask that it be put in layman's terms and if the contract deals with homes or loans I would say hire a lawyer just to be on the safe side. I said that to introduce you to owner financing. Owner financing also known as seller financing, is just that. Instead of borrowing a loan from the bank the seller loan you the money and add-on interest. Some seller's may request a down payment which is fair but it is better than a down payment plus closing cost. In the case of buying through owner's financing allow the owner to write the contract then allow your lawyer to review the contract and voice your expectations and wants to your lawyer to ensure the contract benefit you. Just because the contract is written does not mean you are committed. You can opt out at any time before you sign your name. Scan the contract for fees, monthly payments, interest rate, consequences in cases of late payments, and anything that my affect you negatively. Another way to acquire a home and possibly help a friend or family member is to work out an agreement with a friend or family member who are on the verge of losing their home. As I said, write up an air tight agreement with your lawyer that protects you and your assets, you can take over the payments and become the owner of the property. The individual that was in jeopardy of losing the home benefits from filing bankruptcy, ruining their credit score and chances of buying another home, and escapes paying for that home until they get a buyer. In these cases, be sure that the deed is turned over to you and the proper paperwork is filed. If perhaps you are the one on the edge of losing your home here are a few options: 1. If you have a family, move into a smaller apartment and allow the siblings to share rooms for a while, rent your home out for enough to cover the mortgage on your home to avoid losing it. Now, you're thinking, well what am I getting out of this. You get to keep your home for one. Secondly, if you calculate things correctly, you get to save money to pay your rent and double your mortgage payments to catch up and get a grip on things. Be sure to inform your renter of the short term living arrangements unless you decide to continue rent and purchase another home. 2. If you live alone, getting a roommate is an option. You may not want to but desperate times cause for desperate measure. Your goal is to keep your home so stay focus, problems are only temporary, get a hold of your finances and give a 30-day notice. Be sure to write an air tight agreement each time and know your rights as it concerns renting and allowing people to stay with you. The laws are different in every state.

Now, we can discuss the homes for low to no cost. In every city, there is a Sheriff's tax sale. Contact the Sheriff's office and tell them that you are interested in the sheriff's tax sale and they will redirect you to the proper place just in case it's called something different in your town. At the Sheriff's tax sale, you get a number to bid on a property you want, and once you get the property are only responsible for the taxes on the property for three years. Again, you cannot touch the property yet, you invested the taxes and will have to pay the taxes for three years before the property is legally yours. Within the three years the owner can at any time come and buy the property back from you. Nevertheless, you get your investment plus 17% interest each month that the property was in your possession. For instance, you bought a property for $195 dollars and you had the property for 2 years and 6 months then you received a letter stating that the owner has purchased the property back. Not long after, you will receive a check for $195 dollars plus 17% interest each month they did not buy the property back, so within in this time frame you paid $195 at the auction, $195 at the end of the two years but you will get a return of $994.50. You've paid only $585. You will receive a check for $994.50 so your profit is $409.50. It's a safe and inexpensive investment, and if you invest enough we could move our people out of governmental housing. Now, the catch 20/20 to buying tax sale properties is being knowledgeable of the property you are buying. One thing you do not want to do is buy a property that belongs to a drug dealer because if something is left in the house once they get out of jail, they will come back to get it. You do not want to buy a property with a lien on it. You will be responsible for the debt. You do not want to buy a property that you cannot make a profit from. Build a relationship with someone in the department, and be sure to research, research and research again especially if you don't know the area in which your buying. Let the government keep their apartments, when you get your own you will not have to worry about your rent going up just because you got a raise. Live below your budget. Instead of resources, they gave us welfare but we do not have to keep taking their assistance. You can also consider adjudicated properties. However, most states require you to create an account on the city's website first. Adjudicated property is property that has been turned over to the local government or state due to debtor refusing to pay property taxes. The difference with the adjudicated properties is that the governmental bodies sell their tax interest on the property and the buyer take possession then rather than having to wait three years. Rent to own properties are a rip-off.

Most rent to own properties require that you rent for 15 years before you are eligible to buy the property. Let me iron this out, 15 years and your rent is $650 a month, hypothetically speaking. A home for $85,500 dollar with 4% down payment ($3,420) and a 15-year fixed loan program will cost you approximately $649 a month give or take with the interest rate and PMI. So, with what you are paying them you have bought one home for $85,500 and 15 years, but you must purchase it a second time if you choose to rent to own. Don't waste your time or money with a rent to own property. Don't be fooled by the scams and the fast-talking brother in the suit, green money change minds and you make the rules when it comes to where you spend your money. If they are not willing to bargain find someone that will, do not settle.

HEALTH

Growing up I would rarely hear about people passing, and if I did, the person was very old or killed. Nowadays all I hear is someone dying of cancer or some type of illness. It is very slim chances of someone passing of old age anymore. I started to ponder, and the only thing that has changed is the food we eat and the water we drink. The chemicals that they use to increase products due to supply and demand and pure greed I believe is harmful to us. The lime and other poison's in the water that we bath in, use to brush our teeth, wash our hair in, and drink is harmful to us. Although, there is a cure for most of the disease's we are diagnosed with if you not a millionaire, you cannot afford them. Cancer is the most common disease now, but it has a billion-dollar cure. Let's become more health conscious and increase our life span, longevity has its' place as Dr. King stated, let's place it on our years.

As health conveys to eating, you should eat at least 6 small meals a day, you should eat every 2 hours. Milk is not good for us and when it comes to dairy if you have issues with your lungs dairy product causes mucus build up. Fast food restaurants are not your friend, although the calories are posted, it's not the calories that send you to the hospital it's the preservatives in the food that is unhealthy. The most recent research stated that tilapia is unhealthy because it is a man-made fish. I cannot believe I am about to say this as much as I love sweets, stay away from sugar. There are healthy ways to make ice cream, cookies, brownies, muffins and every other sweet you may want to eat. I am sure you've heard this all before as these are basic health tips. Exercise is essential to the muscles, joints, and range of motion. 30 minutes of walking a day plus healthy eating can result to losing one pound a week. Please keep in mind that stress can lead to weight gain as easy as it can lead to weight loss. If your thing is watching calories, know that 3500 calories equals one pound. So, if you cut your diet by 500 calories a day in 7 days you will lose one pound. Dieting is a hard task, the reason people that diet soon gain all the weight all back, because they deprive themselves of so much and when the diet is over they binge eat. But, if you make healthy eating a lifestyle it wouldn't be so hard to do.

  A holistic health approach is taking a more natural routine to healing versus continuously taking medicine. It is the basic intake of herbs at its natural state to treat non-threatening issues. For illustration, if you are cramping due to your menstrual cycle instead of taking an ibuprofen cut back on sweets and caffeine that should lessen the cramps. Turmeric is a natural herb that helps with inflammation, eases pain, detoxifies your liver, helps you with your stomach, heals flu and colds. My healthy eating guru, Sherriel Miller, has a drink she makes she calls golden milk, it consists of almond milk, turmeric, coconut oil, black pepper, ginger; add honey and or cinnamon for flavor. I'm not going to sell you a dream like I tried it, in fact when it comes to healthy eating I stick to the basis because my taste buds are not matured enough to eat or drink half of the things they say try but I've changed a lot at my own pace. Remember, just because it says organic does not mean that it is organic. The word organic nowadays is a marketing strategy, they just using it to get a sell. Detoxing your liver, lungs, kidney, and colon is very good to do, especially if you take a lot of medicine. No, I'm not saying stop taking prescribed medicine, that's not what I'm saying because your doctor knows best. I am saying if you take medicine such as Tylenol, Aleve, ibuprofen, and etc then you should try a more natural remedy. Detoxify your body in that order, the liver, lungs, kidney, then colon. Most people prefer the one time whole body cleanse and that is fine too. Cascara Sagrada is a good colon cleanser, you take one before bed every night for one week, please check with your physician before taking anything. Although, it is natural, it may conflict with some medicines that you already take. I must forewarn you that it makes you cramp a little but if it is unbearable stop taking them immediately. Bone broth is also good for you. It tastes horrible. But the collagen in bone broth heals your gut lining and reduces intestinal inflammation. It's rich in minerals and support the immune system. I would advise you to research some recipes for taste. Let's start taking more care of our bodies and monitoring what we put in our bodies.

EDUCATION

Education is the most questionable subject I've ran across, yet it is the most potent subject ever when success is mentioned. America loves initials behind your name, and care more so for the initials behind your name than in front of your name. For that reason, on my email signature I purposely leave out the Ms. in front of my name but I be sure to place the M.S. after my name. My friend asked me why and I informed her that the Ms. in front was given to me by default, people can be disrespectful and disregard that but the M.S. at the back, I worked for that and I earned it. No one can disregard that. They may disregard the college I attend, but they cannot deny the knowledge I gained. To those who down play my university, I remind them quickly that college is a place you go to enhance a skill or skills you already obtained. If you attend college looking for a foundation because you skated through grade school then you are twice behind before you start. College is not a place to learn a wide range of knowledge. College is to enhance what you know, and teach you the proper way to use that skill. I acquired a degree in Therapeutic Recreation, which taught me the proper way to assist individuals with disabilities using recreation as a tool to help function socially, emotionally, cognitively, physically, and spiritually to achieve a better quality of life. My second degree in Sports Administration, which specialized in marketing, business, entry level accounting, and education as it pertains to the sports world. Not one of my professors stopped to teach me about life choices, finance or health on a personal spectrum. The information I attained from the lectures were essential to the major I chose only. I was self-reliant and I held myself accountable for what I needed to know to be successful. It goes back to what my grandmother told me, if you only study what the teacher tells you, you will always be the student and they will always be the teacher.

I really want to speak with my mother's about education because I know that a mother's joy is her child's success. My mother and grandmother are proud peacocks when it comes to my success. I want to help make sure we clear a path of success for our children as that is our job. Even if they do not choose the path we paved, we have given them options. I want to introduce you to another investment; this investment is for the sake of the child's future. ESA's (Education Saving Account) is any combination of investments such as mutual funds, stocks, bonds, money market funds, and etcetera. Research the best options for your situation and get advice from your banker and/or financial advisor. If you have more than one child, you can spread what you can afford amongst your children. Also, other's may contribute to the account. Now, I know you may not be able to put thousands of dollars aside to send your child to school, so I want to simplify this the best way I know how. First question, do you have a car note with a payment plan over 48 months? Chances are you couldn't afford that vehicle so they stretched the payments to 60 months or maybe 72 months to bring the payments down. Nevertheless, you end up paying more because of the interest the loan accruals if you are not sending in at least two payments a month to apply towards the principle. Second question, are your payments more than 10% of your income? If so, again chances are you couldn't afford the vehicle. Conversely, you bust your back to make payments to impress people that do not like you. My point is take that car back and get something you pay off within 48 months. Then, bust your back to give your child a future. If you can bend over backwards for a car that gives you no return and is only a liability then why can't you bust your back for your child's future? $20,000-dollar car with a good credit score and 0% APR rate for 24 months will require at least $278 a month without the down payment. A down payment works towards your monthly note, for every $1000 dollars it's $20 off the car note. $20,000 car with a APR rate of 15% comes to $23,000 dollars not including the taxes and title and you put $5000 down because you just got your income tax, so that $5000 just took your payments down $100 dollars. Now, the car is $22,900 and you are on a 72-month payment plan, this will make your payments $318.06 a month give or take after including taxes and title. College for in-state students a year at Grambling State University is $14,126 if you live on campus. So, 4 years without a scholarship is approximately $56,504 dollars. Let's say you started your child ESA when they were 6 years old, you have 12 years which is $22,900 twice that will equal out to $45,800. You would only need an additional $10,704 dollars which is a much better debt than $56,504. I am not saying be without a car, I am saying that we should prioritize and invest in our children future. Don't follow the Jones' with the luxury cars, shop within your budget and be intentional. If you make the decision to have a child, set up a path that gives them the opportunity to be successful. I heard a white man say, "no I don't think that blacks are dumb or ignorant, it's just that blacks do not invest in their children. They value materialistic things." I could not argue that. He told the truth. Majority of us prefer things and never once think about our children furthering their education. Once you save that $45,800 dollars and your child decides not to attend college, you have the option to pay cash for your car. You also have the opportunity to invest in your childs' business or a business of your own. You cannot go wrong when you save money. Another way to save money is to graduate in a major that will pay you for graduating, for example, graduating in teaching in the state of Louisiana if you teach at least 5 years in an urban area than you will be considered for %100 loan forgiveness. Also, if you work for or own a nonprofit with a 501c3 tax exempt status then you are eligible for student loan forgiveness.

Should I force my child to attend college or should I allow them to choose? College is not for everybody, and as bad as we may want our children to go to college and excel sometimes that's not the best route for them. College is a part of the American Dream, something we were never included in. We were never in mind when they mentioned school, college graduate, great job, and a house on the hill with a picket fence. The only place they envisioned us was in the fields or working in the houses. College is not the only way to success, there are several paths to take and paths that can created. If my child had a good plan, I mean a legitimate plan on paper that showed that it was realistic and tangible, I would not force him/her to attend college. Ultimately, without a scholarship or grant the child would only be entering debt. The normal college graduate without a scholarship usually enters the world at least $30,000 dollars in debt. But if your child does not have a skill or trade that they could make a living from, I would give them the pros and cons of incoming the workforce without a degree. In the workforce, a degree is needed to compete for jobs, and not having a degree most times is a way for you to disqualified before even completing an application. My point is to be intentional. A lot of people go to college with no clue of what they want to do and waste much time and money because this is what they thought could get them a good job. On that same note, some people go to college with intent and great plans and lose focus or graduate and cannot find a job because the industry is requesting 5 years of experience or your overqualified because I've been told both. In fact, I went to college lost and declared my major undecided for two semesters. I soon found an area that interested me and planned for success. But that was my journey, my parents did not force me to continue or quit. They allowed me to make the best decision for me. You cannot run their race for them, but you can wait at every pit stop to encourage, support, and love them through it all. Education is so critical in America because a picture is painted that if you do not go to school, it is almost impossible to become successful. Yet, they will back door the barriers placed in front of you and hire someone with a high school diploma because experience outweighs education. This to me is the main reason we must build a relationship with our children, to provide options for them and to know them well enough to be the best supporter you can be. Do not allow anyone to place you or your child in a box. We are a creative people and we almost always think outside the box.

Finally, I am not telling you that these are the only ways to build a foundation, as we all know, there is more than one way to skin a cat. There is HUD.gov for housing counseling, who is also paid to assistance citizens with credit card debt for free. There is State Housing Authority NCSHA.org. They assist with making homes affordable for low-to-moderate income families. There is studentaid.ed.gov/repay-loans, to help you with your student loans, and assist you with loan forgiveness option. There is career one stop center, servicelocator.org to assist with looking for jobs and/or finding unemployment money. There is Small Business Association to assist with starting your own business for free, *www.asbdc-us.org*. There is the Department of Energy Weatherization Assistance Program to assist with energy cost for low-income households, they improve your home to save you money on energy. There is the Crime Victim Compensation program. They assist victims and families of victims with burial cost in case of a murder, rape victims, victims of domestic violence and in some states victims of burglary. There is the program that provide you with a vehicle if you have a job but no car for work,

www.vehicleforchange.org, www.workingcarsforworkingfamilies.org, www.waystowork.org and many others. You can also google, ways to work and search your state. The program in Louisiana is located in Lake Charles. There are plenty programs designed to assist, but if you do not have a clue than you will not look for assistance.

My focal point is our youth, especially knowing that juvenile facilitates rake in at least $3000 a month per child in the State of Louisiana. They are getting rich from placing our children in juvenile facilitates while we struggle to offer programs to decrease deterred behavior. It amazes me that the government will pay so much per child but I formed a nonprofit in Tallulah and I was told that there are no funds in Louisiana. In case I forgot to mention, Tallulah, La is primarily black and it is the home of two state detention centers, one for men and one for women, a jail, and a juvenile facility. In Tallulah, there is absolutely nothing for the youth and young adults, no recreation center, no boys and girls club, no summer jobs, nothing. It staggers me to look at the picture that is being painted, but nevertheless, the portrait is detailed and laid out in black and white. They repetitively say, "we cannot bring anything there because of the crime rate, people are afraid to invest money into the town". What can you offer a child that has lost all hope and only envision a future of selling drugs, robbing, and prison? You offer them love, you offer them support, and you've just gained a relationship that will allow you to reach places that others cannot and you redirect the youth through leadership, through assistance, and through explanation. By explanation, everyone that has gone through tough experiences in life want to know why me, that is an opportunity to ministry to their soul. Now, we do not have time to do this because we are too busy working two or three jobs to buy more stuff. Live below your budget so that you can enjoy your life and spend time with your child. Time is more valuable than those Jordan's you bring in every Saturday. My goal is to share information to enhance what some may know and make others aware and knowledgeable. We constantly ask these entertainers, athletes, and artist for money, we shun them for not investing in the community, yet the community is not in a position to move forward once the funds are received. We have great ideas, however, if you have not planned properly, discipline, or financial savvy, an idea is just an idea. No one invest in ideas. People invest in well thought out dreams that has been put into writing and strategically explained to the investor in a way that he/she plainly see a return or a greater good. One thing about hard work, determination, and ambition it is not hereditary, and all the money in the world cannot purchase it. Nothing can stop us, PRAYED all the way up!

Work Cited

GENE DEMBY (2013). The Truth Behind The Lies Of The Original 'Welfare Queen'. Charles Knoblock/Associated Press.

Laura Green (1998-99). Stereotypes:
Negative Racial Stereotypes and Their Effect on Attitudes Toward African-Americans. Vol. XI, No. 1 Winter.

Boskin, J. (1986). Sambo: The rise and demise of an American jester. New York: Oxford University Press.

Beckner, Chrisanne (2005). People who Changed American History. 100 African Americans who changed history. Wisconsin: World Almanac Library.

Browder, A. T. (1992). Exploding The Myths Vol. 1: Nile Valley Contributions to Civilization. Washington, DC: The Institute of Karmic Guidance.

Must Reads

- Great Moments in Black History by Lerone Bennett Jr.
- From Babylon to Timbuktu by Rudolph R. Windsor
- Before the Mayflower: A History of Black America by Lerone Bennett Jr.
- What Manner of Man by Lerone Bennett Jr.
- Succeeding Against The Odds by John H. Johnson and Lerone Bennett Jr.
- Atlas of the Transatlantic Slave Trade by David Eltis and David Richardson
- Creole New Orleans: Race and Americanization by Joseph Logsdon and Arnold Richard Hirsch
- Post Traumatic Slave Syndrome by Dr. Joy DeGruy-Leary
- 100 Years of Lynching by Ralph Ginzburg
- Breaking Rank by Norman Stamper

In loving Memory

Willie Ann Bosby-Wilmore

Ernest Wilmore, Sr

Carolyn Vee Phillips

Roy Wilmore, Sr

Inez Levels Wright

Percy Wright, Sr

Vera Lee Alexander Wells-Simon

Louis Wells, Sr

Bruce Baines, Sr

Ruby Harris

Printed in the USA
CPSIA information can be obtained
at www.ICGtesting.com
LVHW021046210823
755816LV00011B/566